REVOLUTION
The Making of the Beatles' White Album

Also available in this series:

Not necessarily stoned, but beautiful
The making of *Are You Experienced*

REVOLUTION
The Making of the Beatles' White Album

David Quantick

Published by Unanimous Ltd
12 The Ivories, 6–8 Northampton Street, London N1 2HY

A CIP catalogue record for this book is available from the British Library.

Series editor: Nicola Birtwisle
Text editor: Ian Fitzgerald

ISBN: 1 903318 55 6

Printed in China

2 3 4 5 6 7 8 9

Picture credits
Picture section page 1: Henry Grossman/Timepix/Rex Features. 2 top: Pictorial Press; bottom:
Bozzacchi/Rex Features. 3 top and bottom: Rex Features. 4 top: © Hulton Archive; bottom: Michael
Ochs Archives/Redferns; 5 top and bottom: Rex Features; 6 top: Pictorial Press; bottom: K
Ferris/Pictorial Press; 7 © Bettmann/CORBIS; 8 Rex Features.

contents

introduction

First there is a mountain, then there is no mountain,
then there is a mountain.

Buddhist proverb

IN 1968, THE WORLD'S MOST IMPORTANT POP GROUP had been together for ten years. They would remain together for less than two more. The story is overtold now: even unborn children know, at some deep genetic level, how Paul McCartney met John Lennon at Woolton Fete and showed him some chords. People in remote island communities have heard how the school skiffle group the Quarrymen evolved into the church hall-playing Beatles; how repeat visits to the hard clubs of Hamburg made the teenage rock 'n' roll fans into a tough rock group. Everyone everywhere knows how the greasy rockers who lived on steak and prescription speed were molded by Brian Epstein into teatime pop favorites. And universities now teach courses on how the respectable band members who were able to mix with royalty became drug-using psychonauts who pushed the barriers of popular music so far back that they collapsed.

By 1968, this story was nearly over. Few bands have had such an accelerated lifespan as the Beatles. In short spaces of months, they went through wrenching career changes that would have exhausted other, lesser bands. Since 1963, the band had embraced, reinvented, and often rejected rock 'n' roll, beat pop, country and western, Indian, soul, psychedelia, acid rock, and, from time to time, music hall.

The Beatles of 1968 were not the band they had been even three years earlier. They had rejected live performances for an extended life in studios. They had not immediately replaced their manager, and they no longer seemed to want to be each other. The *Help!*-induced image of the Fabs as four clones in one big house was collapsing. George Harrison, and then John Lennon, would soon release solo albums. Old, apparently solid romantic relationships were collapsing too, as McCartney failed to marry the photogenic actress Jane Asher and Lennon's marriage to Cynthia ossified in Essex.

A casual 1962 Beatles fan would have found it hard to recognize the four members six years later. They did still resemble each other to some extent, but the hair was even longer, and now covered most of the face (McCartney had buried his cocker spaniel cuteness under some kind of sheriff's beard) as if to say, we are grown-ups now. The clothing was radically different. Instead of Pierre Cardin collarless suits, the Beatles dressed like stagecoach travelers in the Wild West—Lennon and McCartney favored black waistcoats, Harrison sported cowboy denim, and Starr still seemed to be getting as much wear as possible out of his 1967-vintage Mr. Fish suits. Most significant of all, the Beatles seemed thinner—Harrison ascetically so, Lennon alarmingly so, as he had always been the band's pie-eater. In 1964, the Beatles had been four aspects of one unit—so much so that writer, broadcaster, opera director, satirist, and all around top brain Dr. Jonathan Miller had been moved to say, "There is something magical and sinister about repetitive siblings . . . the Beatles inspire terror, awe, and reverence. And with that hair they reminded me of the Midwich Cuckoos.

I had no idea they looked so similar—just marginal differentiations on an identical theme." Quite. (With a greater gift for snappiness, Mick Jagger had called the Beatles "the Four-Headed Monster.") In 1968, however, the Beatles no longer resembled clones hatched from a single collarless egg, but four distinct individuals who sometimes used the same tailor. Leaving their 20s with some speed, the Beatles may sometimes have looked like the Band (the hippest, rootsiest group of the year), but they didn't look like *a* band.

True, they were still the biggest group in the world but, like that of a mountain, their huge presence was easy to take for granted. And the Beatles had become as anonymous as the Beatles could get. They were no longer completely lovable. By ignoring the public's mighty whim and not touring, they had lost popular ground. Their obvious fondness for drugs and their interest in unusual religions had alienated the casual fans, as well as the ones who liked it best when they shook their heads and went "woo." Even their movies weren't what they had been. *Magical Mystery Tour*—self-indulgent, incoherent, and not always full of great songs—had achieved the near-impossible feat of making *Help!* look good. More worryingly, the movie had made the band appear short on talent for the first time ever.

Like a mountain, the Beatles were always there. If you lived in London you were always seeing one or another of the Beatles on the street; it was like living in Bombay and seeing sacred cows lumbering past. (If you didn't live in London, you were always seeing them on TV, talking about new labels and new religions and other non-fun stuff.) A few years back, the Beatles had been mobbed on an almost hourly basis.

Now, in 1968, they could walk around town virtually unhindered.

Their dominance of the pop universe was over, too. Other bands had come along—bands with louder guitars who rocked more than the Beatles, bands like Cream and the Jimi Hendrix Experience, who were better at being American, or who were more attractive to teenagers. Seven years is at least two generations in pop terms, and the Beatles had been around, it seemed, since the days before rock. Even their most recent and most awe-inspiring work, *Sgt. Pepper's Lonely Hearts Club Band*, was almost overexposed. The Summer of Love had seen *Sgt. Pepper* imitated by everyone from the Rolling Stones to the Troggs—and even by the Beatles themselves, on the *Magical Mystery Tour* set, which was almost a pastiche of *Sgt. Pepper* (an EP in the United Kingdom, it was extended into a full album in the United States). *Magical Mystery Tour* was toe-tapping rather than world-changing material. The world was finding other things to be getting on with.

Nevertheless, the Beatles were still the Beatles, and a new Beatles album was still a major event. Other groups, even the mighty and evil Rolling Stones, would hold back their album release dates to avoid competing with them. Stores would still clear the shelves of lesser product to make room for the tidal wave of the next Beatles record. They would be number one whatever they did, because they were still the Beatles. It had been more than a year since *Sgt. Pepper*. A new Beatles album was clearly called for. The quartet, apparently absent from music and not caring about working together, reconvened in a moment, as though they had never been away.

First there is a mountain, then there is no mountain, then there is a mountain.

In 1968, the Beatles stopped what they were doing and did what they were best at, which was making a new record. It was the ninth Beatles album, and it would be officially called *The Beatles*, possibly as a step away from the gaudiness of *Sgt. Pepper's* title, possibly to remind the world just whose album this was. As it turned out, nobody in the world has ever called the Beatles' double album *The Beatles*. Instead, it would forever be known by the sensibly elegant and sleeve-based nickname the White Album.

The White Album sits oddly large near the end of the Beatles' career, after the psychedelia and experimentation of their middle period and before the maturity and fragmentation of the final period. It is the band's only double album, the one that contains the most George Harrison songs, and the one that contains the most experimental track the Beatles ever recorded. No singles were taken from it at the time. From its minimalist sleeve—plain white, as the nickname suggests, with a track listing and four portraits of the band—to its poster/lyric sheet, an aptly fragmented collage of Beatle moments and words, the White Album is an extraordinary thing. It contains some of the Beatles' best songs—Paul McCartney's ironic but rocking Beach Boys' pastiche "Back in the U.S.S.R.," George Harrison's epic "While My Guitar Gently Weeps," John Lennon's spooky and near-psychotic "Happiness Is a Warm Gun." It is also the Beatles' most avant-garde album, thanks to the eight-minute sound collage "Revolution 9" (although McCartney's "Honey Pie" and Lennon's own "Good Night" do leaven the album's overall experimentation somewhat).

Even apart from the songs themselves—which, in the case of the Beatles, is a bit like saying "even without everything"— the White Album is a fascinating record. Sprawling and at times unfocused, it's the first Beatles album not to be dominated by George Martin's crisp, clean production, as various band members and engineers did their own production work. More significant, it is an album that has been described as the work of four solo musicians using each other as a backing band. In Beatles history, the White Album was the calm before the split. It was recorded barely a year after Brian Epstein's death, and months after the band's abortive, but calming (and drugless) trip to India. The time of the White Album recordings saw Ringo walk out on, and come back to, the band. Lennon and McCartney worked on different songs in different studios. Most significant, Yoko Ono entered Lennon's life (her brief appearance on Lennon's "The Continuing Story of Bungalow Bill" was the first female vocal ever on a Beatles song). The cold, depressing hell of *Let It Be* was just around the corner.

The White Album is this writer's favorite album by anyone, Beatles or otherwise. There are more succinct Beatles records—*A Hard Day's Night* reflects the band at the summit of their pop songwriting genius, *Revolver* is razor-sharp and arguably the perfect mid-1960s album, *Sgt. Pepper* changed the face of rock—but none of them have the strange quality that the White Album has. It's been argued (and arguers include John Lennon) that it's not a Beatles album at all, but a collection of solo recordings. It doesn't reflect the peak of the band's writing. There are better songs on other albums, and the low points of the White Album are low indeed. In truth, this is a record that could have been subtitled "Farewell, quality control."

Nevertheless, as an album—that is, as a coherent collection of songs that established a mood that is greater than the sum of its parts—the White Album is unsurpassed. From the unbeatable opener, "Back in the U.S.S.R.," via previously unknown worlds of melody and invention, the White Album herds the listener along, barely pausing to acknowledge its seamless gear changes and bomb bursts of jaw-dropping brilliance. On four sides of vinyl, the White Album invented something new in popular music.

Its atmosphere—melancholic, cautionary, sleepy, wise, and angry—is the work of men moving out of their 20s, preparing to leave what Lennon acerbically called "that old gang of mine" for marriage and solo careers. All three songwriting Beatles were entering new phases of maturity as songwriters (and the fourth one actually got a song recorded). Like all great albums, the White Album is both a snapshot of the time it was recorded and a piece of music that stands alone, outside time and fashion. One cannot play *Sgt. Pepper* without thinking of its era; *Revolver* is almost brutally professional; and *Abbey Road* is as sweet and generic as Starbucks coffee. But the White Album stands alone. Of all the Beatles' astonishing records, it's the only one that transcends its "Beatleness," the only one that would be superb if it had been recorded by any other greatest rock and pop band of all time.

The White Album was the sound of the most successful band in the world finally starting to come apart. As that group was the Beatles, they did it with more style and grace than anyone else. Where other groups might have produced messy albums of musical nonsense and despair, the Beatles produced a record that is at turns spooky, funny, exciting, reassuring, avant-garde, traditional, and almost always brilliant. More than thirty years later, the freshness, wit, melody, and experimentation it contained at the time are still present in the same proportions. The White Album is a classic record. And its history, context, and content have proved to be fascinating stories in themselves.

Most books about the Beatles reveal the big picture first and ask questions afterward. This book reverses that approach. *Revolution* looks at the magnificent (and sometimes idiotic) career path of the Beatles through the prism of one vital album; a record, made toward the end of the band's working life, that has been considered by many (including John Lennon) to mark their songwriting peak. It focuses on the intimate recording details and creative processes directly responsible for the White Album. *Revolution* is not so much about "after the fact" as it is *in* the fact, and in the milieu— from the politics, music, culture, and ideas of the era to the band's individual development in the midst of increasing dissolution—that made the White Album not so much possible as inevitable.

1968

"Around 1968, everyone's egos started going crazy."

George Harrison

THERE WERE HINTS THAT 1968 was not going to be a great year for the Beatles. The death of Brian Epstein in 1967 meant that their mentor and unifier, who had already become a fading presence in the band's life, was no longer there to direct their activities and discourage their indulgences. It's hard to say if the White Album might have been a short, snappy collection with no "Revolution 9" or "Wild Honey Pie" on it had Brian Epstein lived. It's more certain that he would have been able to stall *Magical Mystery Tour*. The movie, screened on December 26, 1967, ended the year with critics and fans in a state of enraged bewilderment. Not only did it do a lot to erase the enormous goodwill created by *Sgt. Pepper*, but the movie also served to emphasize the few things about the band that the general public disliked: vagueness, their self-indulgence, and their fascination with India. The Beatles should have gone into 1968 invigorated by the achievement of *Sgt. Pepper*. Instead, they crawled into January managerless, still infatuated with the Maharishi Mahesh Yogi (who had pretty much taken on Epstein's father-figure role), and held in a cautious state of public disapproval.

1968, the year the White Album was recorded, was an extraordinary year, both in the world at large and in the smaller bubble that the Beatles lived in. It was, for starters, a notably violent year. The Vietnam war seemed to change gear, engendering both worldwide revulsion and public protest; the apparent thaw behind the Iron Curtain suffered a major reversal; and Martin Luther King, Jr., and Senator Robert Kennedy were both assassinated. Even the Beatles, who were not exactly hovering on the fringes of public consciousness, were unwillingly moved nearer to the horror when the murderer and maniac Charles Manson used the White Album as a justification for his crimes. The ambiguity and listener-teasing that had become an underground industry for eccentrics would be twisted into something terrible.

In the early days of the Beatles, the events of the world seemed not to enter into the group's songwriting consciousness. The early days of the Vietnam war and the vagaries of the Macmillan Conservative government in Britain weren't likely to crop up in songs like "She Loves You." Even their early "social comment" songs, like "Eleanor Rigby" and "Taxman," were vague on detail and solution ("Taxman" manages to straddle a very big fence by simultaneously blaming both government and opposition leaders for the problem). The *Sgt. Pepper* era and the influence of LSD internalized everything, so that their most outward-looking song of the time was Harrison's "Within You Without You," which advised that change was up to us all.

Despite this, by 1968 the Beatles had acquired a reputation as a group prepared to make pronouncements, vague or otherwise, on the state of life in general. Songs like "All You Need Is Love" were hardly detailed party manifestos, but they were still declarations that many people took seriously. The band had also gotten into the habit of pontificating on broader matters like drugs and spirituality. Without the caution of the early days and a manager to filter questions from the media, the Beatles—John Lennon in particular—were getting into the habit of telling people what they thought, and people were always prepared to listen.

In 1968, as the world seemed to slip away from the haze of peace and love into rioting and unrest, Lennon decided to move the boundaries of social comment away from the dry wit of McCartney's noncommittal songs. While there's a drop of satire but no real political opinion in "Back in the U.S.S.R.," songs such as "Revolution" marked the unveiling of the didactic John Lennon, the one who would fill the early 1970s with statements and sloganeering. "Revolution" is famous for its ambiguities (especially the "count me in/out" line), but, compared to earlier work, it's the first Beatles song to directly engage with the times.

The Beatles' position in the wider world was changing in terms of personal relationships, too, largely because of John Lennon's new love for Yoko Ono. Influenced partly by his quite overwhelming happiness, the desire to use her avant-garde art tactics, and his surrealist humor to promote peace, Lennon, with Ono, went public and Dada on several occasions in 1968. They did so in ways that were polar opposites of the Fab Four comfiness of the mid-1960s. And while the Beatles were managing (so far) to keep their own continental drift out of the papers, internally things were changing. The tensions of the White Album were pushing the band apart. Only the maddest Beatles fanatic could read any significance into the fact that, on the same day in August, Ringo Starr left the band and Cynthia Lennon filed for divorce. Nevertheless, as a starting date for the imminent collapse of the most successful band in the world, August 22, 1968 could hardly be bettered.

The shift in the Beatles' world from the beginning of 1968 to the year's end was also striking. In February, they were all off to Rishikesh to seek enlightenment, wearing Indian garb, wives in tow, seemingly united again. Eight months later, the Beatles were engaging with the business world, writing political songs, fighting off Hell's Angels, and falling apart as a group. For the world and the Beatles, 1967 had seemed to be a golden year. 1968, by contrast, was a very bad year.

January

January 1968 started auspiciously, when on January 5, Alexander Dubcek became the new leader of Czechoslovakia. The hardline nature of the Eastern Bloc, in the pre-détente era, seemed to be softening, and there was some hope that life behind the Iron Curtain would become easier and more liberal. Conversely, at the end of the month, the Viet Cong launched what became known as the Tet Offensive. Named after the Vietnamese religious festival that took place at this time, the Tet Offensive employed some 70,000 North Vietnamese troops and changed the whole tenor of the war in Vietnam. American attitudes about the conflict would change immensely during this time, as more information about U.S. methods used during the war came to light.

The Beatles, like most people, had a quiet January. George spent the 7th to the 12th of the month in Bombay, working with Indian musicians on music for the forthcoming art house film *Wonderwall*, which would star Jane Birkin. He also recorded tracks for one of his best Beatle songs, "The Inner Light," an inevitably spiritual tune.

February

Public attitudes regarding the war in Vietnam were sharply altered after the publication of a picture by American photographer Eddie Adams. Taken on February 1, the photo, which later won the Pulitzer Prize, shows General Nguyen Ngoc Loan, a South Vietnamese security official, executing a Viet Cong prisoner with a gunshot to the head. The image was deeply shocking and did powerful harm to the widely held American notion that the people they were helping were the good guys. Shortly after that incident, an unnamed American major, talking about the Vietnamese town of Ben Tre, which was then under attack, drew attention to American military attitudes by saying, "It became necessary to destroy the town to save it."

On February 2, Richard Nixon entered the New Hampshire primary and declared his presidential candidacy. Nixon had already been defeated by John F. Kennedy, who remained a hated figure to Nixon throughout his life. History, in fact, came to see Nixon as a kind of anti-Kennedy, corrupt and sweaty and weird, where Kennedy was seen as sexy and innocent. History isn't always right.

The Beatles, still full of peace and love, were preparing to visit the Maharishi Mahesh Yogi at his retreat at Rishikesh in Northern India. To give them breathing space career-wise, they spent early February in the studio (around this time, Lennon also seems to have worked on the future White Album song "Cry Baby Cry," and McCartney played drums on a session for former Manfred Mann vocalist Paul Jones.) At Abbey Road, the band worked on four new songs. Two rockers—McCartney's bluesy "Lady Madonna" and Lennon's

"Hey Bulldog"—and two spiritual songs—Lennon's "Across the Universe" and Harrison's "The Inner Light"—were recorded. ("Across the Universe" was put aside for a charity album, and "Hey Bulldog" ended up on the *Yellow Submarine* soundtrack album.) This done, on February 15, the band departed for Rishikesh.

March

On March 16, Senator Robert Kennedy, former Attorney General and brother of John F. Kennedy, announced that he would enter the 1968 Presidential race. Richard Nixon thus found himself once more up against a Kennedy. The same day in Vietnam, American troops massacred over 500 Vietnamese civilians in the village of My Lai.

On March 17, a peaceful protest against the Vietnam War in London's Grosvenor Square turned violent, indicating a change in attitudes about acceptable forms of protest both by the authorities and by the protesters themselves. On March 22, Czech president Antonin Novotny resigned, causing Warsaw Pact leaders to meet the next day and discuss the threat that the increased liberalization of Czechoslovakia posed. At the end of March, U.S. president Lyndon B. Johnson announced that he was not going to stand for re-election and that there would be a halt to U.S. bombing in Vietnam.

While the Beatles were in Rishikesh, on the 15th, "Lady Madonna" was released as a single, backed with "The Inner Light." The former song marked a step away from the band's psychedelic pop direction of 1967, while the latter was an accurate indication of the current state of the Beatles' minds.

In Rishikesh, both Harrison and Beach Boy Mike Love celebrated their birthdays. George was 25, and Love's birthday was commemorated in song by the Beatles in a Beach Boy-ish medley called "Spiritual Regeneration/ Happy Birthday Mike Love." After two weeks of Indian food, the insects that his wife Maureen hated, and, possibly, the company of the not universally popular Mike Love, Ringo and Maureen Starr returned to the United Kingdom. Paul remained in India for two more weeks.

During their stay, which was punctuated by visits from film and television crews, the Beatles, the band Love, and British folk pop singer Donovan were filmed by Italian TV singing an unusual medley of songs. These ranged from "When the Saints Go Marching In" and "She'll Be Coming 'Round the Mountain" to "You Are My Sunshine" and "Jingle Bells," and also included Bob Dylan's "Blowin' in the Wind" and Donovan's own "Catch the Wind." None of the many nascent Beatles songs written during this time were performed for the cameras, even though most of the White Album (and some of *Abbey Road*) was being composed around this time.

April

On April 4, one of the worst moments of the 1960s occurred when Martin Luther King, Jr., was assassinated by James Earl Ray in Memphis, Tennessee. King's murder stunned the world: his brand of nonviolent protest and his commitment to civil rights had impressed millions and brought new hope to people everywhere. His assassination was one of the first events that changed the optimistic tenor of the 1960s, and his absence was instrumental in the rise of more militant black activists such as the Black Panthers. King's death also sparked rioting all over America.

On April 12, John Lennon and George Harrison returned from India. Lennon was deeply disillusioned by the Maharishi's apparent lack of spirituality and his alleged sexual assault on fellow Rishikesh visitor Mia Farrow.

May

On May 6, one of the pivotal events of 1968 took place in Paris. Some 5,000 students marched through the Latin Quarter of Paris, and riots broke out. The rioting, which saw police using gas grenades and students setting up barricades in the old French tradition, went on into the night, and ensured the support of French workers, themselves heavily unionized. From May 13 to May 22, strikes broke out throughout France, and over 9 million workers were involved in strike action. Meanwhile, on the 9th, Soviet troops massed on the Czech border.

The Beatles seemed, at this stage, to be unconcerned about the world situation. On May 14, they launched Apple Corps Ltd. in New York. At the launch, McCartney explained to the world that the Beatles were "hippie capitalists" and set out the band's aim of encouraging artists of all kinds to send them their work. Apple was a generous and optimistic idea, and one that was bravely going ahead despite the failure of the short-lived Apple Boutique on Baker Street in London.

Lennon had other things on his mind at this time, too. On May 18, he called a meeting of the Beatles to tell them— possibly while under the influence of certain hallucinogenic substances—that he was Jesus. On the 19th, he spent the night with Yoko Ono, recording their first collaboration *Unfinished Music No. 1: Two Virgins,* and then making love at dawn.

Shortly after this, the band convened at Harrison's bungalow in Surrey, Kinfauns, and began to record demo songs for their next album. The songs committed to tape at that session that did end up on the White Album were "Julia," "Blackbird," "Rocky Raccoon," "Back in the U.S.S.R.," "Honey Pie," "Mother Nature's Son," "Ob-La-Di, Ob-La-Da," "Dear Prudence," "Sexy Sadie," "Cry Baby Cry," "The Continuing Story of Bungalow Bill," "I'm So Tired," "Yer Blues," "Everybody's Got Something to Hide Except Me and My Monkey," "Revolution," "While My Guitar Gently Weeps," "Happiness Is a Warm Gun," "Piggies," and "Glass Onion." In addition, three Harrison songs—"Sour Milk Sea," "Not Guilty," and "Circles"—were demoed. The former was later recorded by Apple act and fellow Liverpudlian Jackie Lomax, while the latter two were ignored until they were recorded by Harrison much later in his solo career. McCartney's "Jubilee"—later renamed "Junk" and released on his solo album *McCartney*—and Lennon's "Child of Nature"—later rewritten as "Jealous Guy" and released on his solo album *Imagine*—were also demoed.

On May 30, the sessions proper for the White Album began at Abbey Road, with extensive work on the seemingly simple "Revolution 1."

June
On June 3, artist Andy Warhol was shot in New York by Valerie Solanas, an actress and extreme proto-feminist, best

known for writing the S.C.U.M. (Society for Cutting Up Men) Manifesto. Warhol recovered physically, but the mental effects of the shooting and the physical scarring were to make him even more introspective and reclusive than before. Two days later, on the night of the California primary election, Robert Kennedy was shot after addressing supporters at the Ambassador Hotel in San Francisco. His assassin was a 24-year-old Jordanian called Sirhan Sirhan, who was angered by Kennedy's apparent pro-Israeli stance. Coming so soon after Martin Luther King, Jr.'s, assassination, Kennedy's murder fuelled an increasing disillusionment with the effectiveness of idealistic politics.

In spite of—or perhaps because of—recent events, John Lennon went with Yoko Ono to Coventry Cathedral to plant "Acorns for Peace," the first, and least unconventional, of the couple's public peace demonstrations. Lennon also worked on tape loops for a stage production of his book *In His Own Write* at London's Old Vic Theatre. Paul McCartney celebrated his 26th birthday on May 18, and on the 30th, the acclaimed Black Dyke Mills brass band recorded McCartney's instrumental "Thingumybob." George Harrison took up sitar lessons with his mentor Ravi Shankar, and also played on a Jackie Lomax session.

The Beatles as a unit appeared on the Kenny Everett radio show, where they launched into somewhat on-the-spot performances of the Beach Boys' current single, "Cottonfields," and a rendition of the classic "Tiny Tim for President." They continued to work on their new album. Significantly, for the first time, two Beatles worked in two different studios at the same time: Lennon on tape loops for

"Revolution 9," McCartney on an effectively solo recording of "Blackbird." "Blackbird" was one of the songs filmed by Apple as a promotional vehicle on June 11, along with "Helter Skelter" and "Mother Nature's Son."

July

On July 12, riots took place in Los Angeles, adding to the tension of an already long, hot summer. On July 1, John's exhibition "You Are Here"—put together by Yoko Ono and John—opened at the Robert Fraser Gallery in London. To mark its opening, Lennon and Ono released balloons. On July 7, Ringo was 28, and on the 18th the movie *Yellow Submarine* had its launch party. The Beatles appeared in the film for only a couple of minutes at the end, their roles being taken by actors in the main cartoon section, and their musical contributions—two eerie but excellent Harrison offcuts, the epic "It's All Too Much" and the wry "Only a Northern Song," Lennon's scything "Hey Bulldog" and McCartney's daffy "All Together Now"—tended to suggest that the album was not high on their list of concerns (side two was taken up entirely by George Martin's charming orchestral themes). The eventual release of the *Yellow Submarine* album in January 1969 meant that the White Album (which had been preceded by *Magical Mystery Tour*) was a giant record bookended by two slightly downscale soundtracks.

On July 10, the Beatles recorded the fast, rock version of "Revolution." Five days later, Apple Corps moved into 3 Savile Row, and engineer Geoff Emerick quit the White Album sessions. Five days after that, Paul's fiancée Jane Asher announced that their engagement was off. At the end of the month the Apple Boutique closed, the first indicator that the Beatles' "hippie capitalism" might not be working.

Then came a slight hitch in the Beatles' plans for the White Album. The British rock group Family released its album *Music in a Doll's House*, which effectively thwarted the Beatles' original choice of title for their new album: *A Doll's House*.

Between album sessions, there was more solo work for two Beatles. Under the fine pseudonym Apollo C. Vermouth, McCartney produced—and played ukulele on—the Bonzo Dog Doo-Dah Band's "I'm the Urban Spaceman," and, in complete contrast, played guitar on Welsh folk/pop singer Mary Hopkin's "Those Were the Days." Ringo, meanwhile, played drums on a Solomon King session, becoming the first Beatle to perform on a recording of "Hava Nagila." On July 26, the Beatles were filmed rehearsing "Hey Jude" and, on the 30th, they recorded it.

August

On August 8, Richard Nixon was nominated the Republican Party's presidential candidate, and on the 9th he appointed Spiro Agnew as his running mate. On the 20th, 200,000 Warsaw Pact troops invaded Czechoslovakia. The world was suitably horrified but took no action against the invasion, and the Eastern Bloc settled down to nearly 20 years of uninterrupted totalitarianism.

On August 26, the Democratic National Convention began in Chicago. The police, faced with peaceful demonstrations, tried unsuccessfully to enforce an 11:00 P.M. curfew. Tension between police and protestors continued to increase until, on August 28, police attacked a crowd of demonstrators without provocation. The image of the police as "fascist pig oppressors" was suddenly confirmed for hippies and students everywhere, causing further rifts between them and "the establishment." John Lennon and Yoko Ono were moved to comment on the riots: Lennon said, "People should ask what they are rioting for, not against."

The new Beatles album, meanwhile, was not going well. On August 17, having recorded 110 takes of "Not Guilty," a song that never did appear on any Beatles album, George Harrison went to Greece. On August 20, John and Ringo visited one of Paul's sessions, and a notable frost descended until they left again. Two days later, on the day that Cynthia Lennon filed for divorce, Ringo left the band. On August 24, John and Yoko gave a TV interview to David Frost, unveiling their new public persona as outspoken twin Dadaists for the very first time.

During this time, the band also worked on two other songs that were never released on any Beatles album. One was the perhaps deliberately annoying "What's the New Mary Jane," a song that the band would continue to work on in 1969. The other was a McCartney track called "Etcetera," which has never been heard, or heard of, since.

On the 30th, the last great Beatles single was released. The A-side was "Hey Jude" and the B-side was the fast version of "Revolution." "Hey Jude," inspired by John's son Julian Lennon, was famously believed by both Lennon and McCartney to be a song about each other. At that time, it was the longest single ever released, at an epic length of seven minutes and eleven seconds.

September

On September 1, Democratic presidential candidate Hubert Humphrey began his campaign in New York. Two days later, Ringo Starr returned to the Beatles. He found his drum kit bedecked with flowers by George Harrison, as well as a general atmosphere of relief. On the 8th, David Frost screened the now-famous "Hey Jude" clip on his show.

The album sessions continued. On September 18 the band recorded "Birthday," a song whose rock feel was inspired by that night's screening on BBC TV of the classic rock 'n' roll movie *The Girl Can't Help It*. All of the Beatles watched the movie, and felt suitably hopped up by it.

Hunter Davies's Beatles biography came out on the 30th, effectively sealing a whole Beatle chapter by turning years of the band's career into written history.

October

On October 3, independent U.S. presidential candidate George Wallace announced his running mate, former Air Force Chief of Staff Curtis E. LeMay. On October 11, Apollo 7 was launched from Florida. The next day, the Olympic Games began in Mexico City, only ten days after violent student protests that had left many dead. 32 African nations boycotted the games because of South Africa's involvement. On the 18th, U.S. athletes Tommie Smith and John Carlos gave the black power salute during the televised awards ceremony. On October 31, Lyndon Johnson announced a halt to U.S. bombing in North Vietnam.

The Beatles were coming to the end of the White Album recording sessions. On the 9th, McCartney recorded "Why

Don't We Do It in the Road?" with Ringo, while Lennon and Harrison were elsewhere. Lennon expressed regret and sorrow that this had happened, possibly because it happened on his birthday. McCartney later confessed that he recorded the song without Lennon partly as revenge for being left out of "Revolution 9." It was getting to be an increasingly petty Beatle world.

On the 14th, an overdub session for Harrison's "Savoy Truffle" marked the end of 137 days of White Album sessions. Only 16 songs out of 30 featured all four Beatles, one featured the band's first ever female lead vocal (a line on "Bungalow Bill" sung by Yoko Ono), one was an epic avant-garde track, and one ("While My Guitar Gently Weeps") showcased the band's first use of a star guest musician, Eric Clapton. The 16th and the 17th were taken up with an incredible 24-hour running order session, which produced the superb sequencing and track listing that we know today. And, just for the hell of it, the police busted John and Yoko for possession of drugs on the 18th.

During this month, incidentally, McCartney also found time to play guitar on a session by another Apple artist, James Taylor. The 1970s were just around the corner.

November

On November 5, U.S. elections took place. 31,770,000 people voted for Nixon, 31,270,000 for Humphrey, and 9,906,000 for the independent, Wallace. Nixon became president. On November 14, the nation celebrated the new era with National Turn In Your Draft Card Day. On November 26, the South Vietnamese government agreed to join peace talks in Paris.

Beatle life was a varied affair during this month. On November 1, Harrison's movie soundtrack *Wonderwall Music*, the first album to be issued on the Apple label, was released. On November 8, Lennon's divorce from Cynthia Lennon was finalized. On November 21, Yoko Ono suffered a miscarriage. Her first collaboration with Lennon, *Two Virgins*, came out on November 29. Its sleeve, which showed the couple nude, distressed many people, not least of whom was Sir Joseph Lockwood, head of EMI. Many brown paper bags were used in its distribution.

It was a good month for Beatle solo work in general. George Harrison played on two disparate recording sessions. He sang "Nowhere to Go" and "I'd Have You Anytime" with Bob Dylan in Woodstock, and, with Bernie Krause, recorded a synthesized track called "No Time or Space" for his second solo album, *Electronic Sounds*, which would be released in 1969. He also recorded with Jackie Lomax in Los Angeles for Lomax's album *Is This What You Want?*, and he managed to find time to play on Cream's "Badge," a song he co-wrote with Eric Clapton (and produced, under the marvelous name of L'Angelo Misterioso.)

Paul McCartney worked on sessions for Mary Hopkin's album *Postcard*, which included a version of his new song "Blackbird." John Lennon, meanwhile, made several home recordings. Some of these recordings would appear on *Let It Be* ("Don't Let Me Down"; "I've Got a Feeling"), some would appear later as solo recordings ("Look at Me"; "Oh My Love"), and one would never appear on any commercially available recording ever (the hypnotic, slightly scary "A Case of the Blues").

On November 22, the Beatles' ninth studio album, bluntly called *The Beatles*, came out in the United Kingdom (it was released in the United States on November 25). It was the first Beatles album on Apple Records and their only double album. It sold over one million copies in its first five days of release in the United States.

December

December was, thankfully, a quiet month for the world. On the 21st, Apollo 8 was launched. It was the first U.S. spacecraft to orbit the moon.

In Beatle terms, life went on. December 10 and 11 saw the filming and recording of the Rolling Stones' *Rock 'n' Roll Circus* concert at the Lyceum Theatre in London, where Lennon performed "Yer Blues" with Keith Richards, Eric Clapton, and Mitch Mitchell. The song also segued into a Yoko-vocalized version, known variously as "Her Blues" or, perhaps some time after the event, "Whole Lotta Yoko." On December 18, Lennon and Ono took part in the first Bag Event, a concert for peace, at the Albert Hall. On December 7, with some inevitability, the White Album went to number one in the United Kingdom.

the people

"I never made any money out of the Beatles' success. I just got my same EMI salary and never participated in their huge profits. No one could say I rode on the backs of the Beatles."

George Martin

THE BEATLES

Collectively, the Beatles were emerging from an extraordinary year. 1967 saw them make and release two of the most important recordings of their career and of the 1960s: the LP *Sgt. Pepper's Lonely Hearts Club Band*, their most extravagant and atmospheric album; and the unique, double-A-side single of "Strawberry Fields Forever" and "Penny Lane." It was arguably the creative peak of the band's career. Freed from touring, freed from Beatlemania, and freed from convention (don't take drugs, don't take months in the studio), the Beatles went from being the most popular band in the world to being the most important. With *Sgt. Pepper* and its satellite single, the Beatles became more than a very good band. They became a new category of band.

And in 1967, having got as high as possible, in both the literal and artistic senses of the word, the Beatles began to decline. Even the 1967 global live TV broadcast of "All You Need Is Love" was a bit anticlimactic after recent musical events. Lennon sounded washed out, the quotations from "The Marseillaise," bits of "She Loves You," and "In the Mood" were fun but not innovative, and there was a sense of "treading water" about the whole thing.

A search for new ways of thinking led the band to the Maharishi Mahesh Yogi in Bangor, but it also coincided with the death of Brian Epstein, the man who had taken the Beatles away from their German leather rocker, toilet-seat-'round-the-neck origins to the London Palladium, Pierre Cardin suits, and MBEs (a British honor). The Beatles' professional reaction to Epstein's death was to launch themselves into a film project, the confused and indulgent *Magical Mystery Tour*. While at times this film is redeemed by superb music—including "I Am the Walrus," one of the best rock singles of all time—and some genuinely funny moments, *Magical Mystery Tour* became the blueprint for the Bad Rock Movie. Lennon had famously told Brian Epstein to stick to his percentages while the band looked after the music. At this stage in their career, the Beatles should perhaps have just stuck to the music. At the same time, the failure of "Strawberry Fields Forever/Penny Lane" to beat Engelbert Humperdinck's "Please Release Me" to the number one position on the music charts started a flood of "have the Beatles had it?" articles. There was a strange irony to this. The Beatles released the most experimental album of all time, it went to number one all over the world, and everyone asked, "Is it over for the band?" Arguably, it was. As innovators, the Beatles would never be more creative and influential again (brilliant though "Revolution 9" is, it did not herald a new direction for rock music).

The Beatles began 1967 as emperors of pop music and the virtual owners of popular culture, and ended it unfocused, criticized, and unraveled. They may have been all shiny and moustached and uniformed for the cover of *Sgt. Pepper*, but, post-touring and post-drugs, they were clearly individuals now, no longer the four near-clones described by Jonathan Miller. Now they were diffusing like crazy. By the end of 1968, the Beatles' Christmas record would feature Lennon referring acidly to the rest of the band and other people around Ono and himself as "some of their beast friends." Harrison would be musically and mentally turning himself into an American post-Dylan singer-songwriter. McCartney— having announced his engagement to Jane Asher on Christmas Day, 1967—would soon be hurtling toward joyful domesticity with Linda Eastman. Even Starr would be running off, wishing he was an octopus and making solo records.

The visit to the spiritual retreat at Rishikesh offered a way out of this increased separateness. The band members and their wives decamped en masse to the Maharishi's base in India, and, judging by recorded evidence, seem to have genuinely picked up some holiday spirit. Without drugs, without London club life, and without the studio to sit around in, the Beatles did something they hadn't done since the buses and hotels of their touring peak: they sat around and wrote songs on acoustic guitars. Due in part to the rural mystic atmosphere (and to Donovan, who had tagged along as a kind of hippie folk technical adviser), the songs the Beatles were writing were pastoral, melodic, and acoustic (so much so that, when they returned, the band recorded acoustic demos together at George's house, for the first and only time in their career). Rishikesh could have been a great unifier for the Beatles, who might then have produced a relaxed, "natural" White Album, a contrast to the heavy wild psychedelia of 1967. Instead, everything fell apart. In a confused and never properly explained turn of events, the Maharishi was all but accused of rape, and the Beatles returned home, disillusioned again.

Lennon's post-Rishikesh mood is easily discerned from a tape he made for, and with, Yoko Ono upon his return. Over a minimal acoustic backdrop, he half sings, half talks somewhat cattily about how most of the women present resembled schoolteachers, about people ogling swimsuited women instead of meditating—and about Beatle wives being attracted to an actor called Tom. He also sings to Ono that he wrote "600 songs" about his emotional state. Significantly, he tells her that he felt like killing himself, and also that his burst of creativity had nothing to do with the Maharishi. He talks, with more than a hint of jealousy, about one woman going to the Yogi for "private interviews" (Lennon and every-one else had to wait in line for said interviews). Lennon says that the Maharishi appeared to be holy—Ono chimes in, suggesting that he might be a sex maniac—and Lennon adds that, in fact, he might not have been holy after all. How much of this was designed to make Ono feel that she was missed—he sent her postcards every day from Rishikesh—is hard to gauge, but Lennon's ironic disdain runs through the whole recording. It's a massively ironic contrast to the sense of fun and relaxation that makes the throwaway "Spiritual Regeneration/Happy Birthday Mike Love"—recorded while at Rishikesh—so jaunty, and the woozy bliss of "Child of Nature" so appealing. (Not insignificantly, the latter song's lyric was completely abandoned by Lennon, and the melody resurfaced three years later in the form of "Jealous Guy." Even a melody can have an interesting and varied life.)

The sense of Lennon's disillusion while making this recording is strong. There's an often-repeated story of Lennon going up in a helicopter with the Maharishi in the belief that, when they were alone together, the Yogi might "slip him the answer." Cynicism and naivety often being different sides of one coin, it's easy to see how Lennon's excitement at the prospect of being shown something fresh, pure, and innocent could flip over into disgust and contempt when that something turned out to be apparently corrupt.

Paul McCartney took a different approach. Having left Rishikesh after five weeks, he was not present when the alleged near-rape incident took place, and in fact, still does not believe that it happened. McCartney blames the whole thing on Lennon's technical guru and all-around mouthy idiot Alex Mardas. "Magic" Alex was a persuasive (to LSD users) type who wrangled large sums of cash from the Beatles and Apple Corps to make (or, more accurately, fail to make) a variety of exciting and never-produced inventions. Only in the 1960s would internationally famous rock stars as intelligent and experienced as John Lennon and George Harrison believe anything told to them by a man who claimed he had invented wallpaper that played music. (Later, Lennon would be less charitable to Mardas, referring to him publicly as "the mad Greek.") Within hours of arriving in Rishikesh, Mardas was spreading the rumor that the Maharishi had done something appalling. Paul had returned to the United Kingdom with Jane Asher, quite content that he had learned as much as possible from the experience. Subsequently, he was surprised and amused by Lennon's immensely self-righteous anger at the Maharishi (Lennon, after all, had spent the flight home from India drinking and telling his wife how many lovers and prostitutes he had slept with).

Harrison was, like Lennon, confused by Alex's assertions, but he came down on the Maharishi's side. He continued his love of transcendental meditation right up until his death, from the Hari Krishna backing vocals on "My Sweet Lord" to chanting the same mantra when he was attacked on New Year's Eve, 1999.

Ringo Starr, who'd left Rishikesh early, seemed unaffected by the allegations against the Yogi, and even provided the best quote about the whole experience. He said it was "like Butlins" (a British "holiday camp," part economy vacation resort and part boot camp). In the early 1960s, Starr was a musician at Butlins, and returned there in the 1970s to play the part of David Essex's only friend in the superb British rock movie *That'll Be the Day*.

After Rishikesh, the Beatles effectively found themselves right where they had been three months previously—fragmented, bad-tempered, and diverse. In 1968, the Beatles were not so much on the decline as they were approaching the jumping-off point for their lives as solo artists and, to coin a phrase, as men.

Ringo Starr

Ringo Starr had always been a self-contained unit. Independent and far from extroverted after a long childhood illness, peritonitis, had caused him to spend a year in hospital, Starr had always been his own man. As a drummer, he was not involved in the compositional and ideas process of the Beatles, and spent much of *Sgt. Pepper's* recording time playing cards in the studio. As a star, he was branching out and making appearances in films, first in *Candy* and later in *The Magic Christian*. Starr was unaffected by the surface changes in the band, whether they were the musical upheavals of *Sgt. Pepper* or the spiritual quest to Rishikesh. When he eventually came to record his first solo album it was, unsurprisingly, not a set of avant-garde tape loops or Indian sitar excursions, but a collection of prewar golden oldies designed to please his mum, with a photo of the pub at the end of Ringo's street in Liverpool on the front cover.

Paul McCartney

Like Starr, McCartney never let either his independence or his fondness for the conventional be overwhelmed by events. Despite his interest in the avant-garde—he still maintains, with some annoyance, that he was the first "Art Beatle," both supporting the Indica Gallery and championing bad-tempered composer Karl-Heinz Stockhausen—McCartney's primary concern was the Beatles. And McCartney's perception of the Beatles was very close to the public's perception of the Beatles: a musical, inventive, successful unit who wrote great songs and were the best at what they did. Despite his enormous talent, McCartney always seemed to sense that the band was the best vehicle for his abilities. He seemed to need a Lennon off whom to bounce ideas, or even a group of people to restrain his boundless enthusiasms. More likely, he just enjoyed the security of a group to hide behind and to showcase his abilities. Able to record "solo" songs while in the Beatles—"Yesterday" being his most famous—Paul's idea of a solo project was always non-group threatening, whether it was a film soundtrack (*The Family Way*) or a TV show theme song ("Thingumybob").

After Brian Epstein's death, however, McCartney found himself in an uneasy position. He wanted the group to go on, but nobody else seemed to want to hold it together. Instead of stepping back and perhaps letting the Beatles dissolve, McCartney opted to become group leader. Over the next two years, he wrote the majority of Beatles singles—"Lady Madonna," "Hey Jude," "Let It Be," and (in the United States) "The Long and Winding Road"—-and would eventually, and unwittingly, lead the band into the hell of the *Let It Be* project. Unaffected by the "unmasking" of the Maharishi, keen to keep the group's momentum going (a master of the single, he was a natural to write "Lady Madonna," the "stopgap" single released during the Rishikesh trip), Paul McCartney was probably the most enthusiastic supporter of the next Beatles project. The Beatles were, after all, his day job.

George Harrison

For Harrison, the Beatles were about to become an annoyance. McCartney's positioning of himself as group leader, coupled with his desire to control his own songs, meant that Harrison was in danger of becoming a session guitarist in his own band. Harrison was also burgeoning as a songwriter, which hadn't always been the case. Lennon and McCartney—competitive, prolific, and perhaps the best songwriters in the world—were dismissive of his songs, and Harrison would always come third on any Beatles album (sometimes, like Ringo, he would even be reduced to singing one of John and Paul's songs). But by 1968, Harrison had two new sources of creative strength. Musically, he was leaning away from the Beatles' supreme pop toward both Bob Dylan's acoustic sound and the similar directions of West Coast rock. Thematically, he had something different to write songs about, too. From the epic essay of "Within You Without You"—surely the most considered and reasoned Beatles lyric—to the comparatively snappy Krishna pop of "The Inner Light," Harrison was about to become the most famous proselytizer of Eastern religion. As the only Beatle to seriously concern himself with spiritual matters after the Rishikesh affair, Harrison's faith would inform the rest of his life.

George Harrison approached the White Album at a time when his Beatle identity had been partly replaced by his new, more spiritual, individuality, and when he was also becoming more of an individual songwriter. In a year's time, he would actually have his first A-side on a Beatles' single—the classic "Something." Even in 1968, however, he was writing unique and distinctive songs. Some were Beatle-like, and some displayed Harrison's more idiosyncratic tendencies, but all fit within the White Album's slightly ironic, sideways sprawl of ideas. Harrison may have had more songs on the White Album simply because there was so much time to fill, but his work there is among his best on a Beatles record.

John Lennon

Lennon had begun his Beatle life angry, motherless, violent, and married to someone he had made pregnant. Through the band's career, he had subdued his rage and obsessive urge for "honesty" (with its flipside, brutal blunt cruelty) to become the sardonic Beatle. From the quips about jewelry-rattling at royal concerts and the Lennon camera leer, he also became known as the Smart Beatle, the one who wrote books and wore Bob Dylan hats. After the band stopped touring, his imagination—encouraged (or hindered) by LSD and marijuana—ran wild. By his own account, Lennon seemed to spend most of the mid-1960s saying "Why not?" to people who told him the Beatles couldn't record a seven-minute song or sound like an orange. Musically freed, away from the Beatlemania public, off his head on drugs, Lennon was also about to meet the woman who would both mold his personality and collaborate on his work for the rest of his life. This would end a marriage that had lasted the length of the band's career, and push his urge for truth-telling and seeing things "the way they are" (at the expense of seeing things the way they might be) to the forefront. It would create the frank, stripped-down, political, feminist, drunk, and, finally, loved and loving John Lennon—the one who, partly because of his murder and partly through the sheer force of his personality—became the only Beatle to achieve icon status in his post-Beatle years.

At the time of the White Album, however, Lennon had not embarked on a sexual affair with Ono and was still flirting with her via art exhibitions, cute conceptual gags, and postcards. He still lived with Cynthia out in Weybridge, and was still deeply unhappy with his life. Escapism through extramarital sex, drugs, and work was not enough. With the death of Brian Epstein and the disillusionment with the Maharishi, Lennon should have been a man suspended in apathy in the spring of 1968. Instead, he was about to embark on the most important relationship of his adult life.

Yoko Ono

A book about the Beatles would be incomplete without some words on Yoko Ono. More than any other of the Beatles' partners, Ono exerted a major influence on the group, favorably in Lennon's case and less so in respect to the rest of the group. As an artist and as an individual, she affected both Lennon's life and the course of the White Album, and her life and influence before and after the Beatles are deeply relevant here.

Yoko Ono was born on February 18, 1933, in Tokyo. Her father was a banker, and her mother was from the rich, patrician family that had founded the Yasuda Bank. Ono's father had worked in New York and San Francisco. The Onos were a privileged and well-off family, to say the least. Yoko did not meet her father until she was two and a half years old. Having been transferred to San Francisco six weeks before she was born, Eisuke Ono didn't meet his own daughter until Yoko and her mother joined him in California in 1935.

Ono was an isolated child. Later she would tell people how, as a child, she would ring for tea just so a maid would come and she would have someone to talk to. Her main contact with the outside world, aptly enough, was as a performer. She gave her first piano recital at the age of four.

At the end of the war, Ono and her mother and siblings briefly found themselves refugees, begging for food in the Japanese countryside. Back in Tokyo and reunited with their father, her life took on another surreal aspect as she found herself at school with Emperor Hirohito's two sons—she shared a class with the Crown Prince Akihito, whose younger brother, Yoshi, had a crush on Yoko. The family eventually returned to the United States, moving to Scarsdale, New

York, where Ono continued the classical piano training she had begun in Japan, and started writing prose and poetry. Ono had already attended college in Japan, becoming the first woman to study philosophy at her university, and at 20, she went to Sarah Lawrence College—oddly, the same college that Linda McCartney would later attend.

Yoko's main interest at this time was the musical avant-garde, especially Schoenberg and John Cage. In defiance of her parents, she married one of her fellow students, Toshi Ichiyanaga. In 1956, the couple moved into a New York City loft, which became the location for several early 1960s performance events, hinting at elements of Ono's later career.

In 1962, Ono returned to Japan, divorced Ichiyanaga, and married American film producer Anthony Cox. A year after the birth of their daughter Kyoko, the couple returned to New York, where Ono, funded by Cox, continued to explore avant-garde art. She had become associated with the Fluxus movement—a group of artists now ironically best known for being associated with Yoko Ono—whose work, antitraditional and a reaction against the abstract painting style that was dominant at the time, was also public, sensational, and media-oriented. Fluxus was also funny, an aspect that may well have originated with Ono, whose performance pieces included banging her head on a floor, making daft and wry statements, and, more scarily, *Cut Piece*, in which she invited the audience to cut the clothes off her body. This latter piece led to her being invited to mount an exhibition in London. On November 9, 1966, at a preview for the show, Yoko Ono met John Lennon.

There was an instant attraction between Ono and Lennon, but it was not purely sexual. Lennon saw something of his own surreal sense of humor in Ono's work. He also admired the optimism of her *Yes Painting*—the viewer had to climb a ladder to read the word "Yes." Ono's work was also conceptual, and not as obscure and elitist-seeming as was much of contemporary art. It was accessible and comprehensible. McCartney already had his Stockhausen and his Magrittes; now Lennon had his own avant-garde interest. He funded Ono's 1967 show *Yoko Ono Plus Me*, which largely consisted of household items cut in half and painted white—the latter motif an Ono/Lennon constant, from Lennon's white suit on the cover of *Abbey Road* to the white "Imagine" piano, until 1972.

In her own right, Ono also performed with avant-jazzer Ornette Coleman at the Albert Hall, tied herself to the Trafalgar Square lions, and—most famously of all—made the film *Bottoms*, which featured 365 bottoms winking away at the camera for two hours. Described, memorably, by Ono as "an aimless petition signed by people with their anuses," *Bottoms* is a charming, if slightly too long, movie, and its humor—its cheek, as it were—has often been overlooked by people who wouldn't know a joke if it bit off their noses. Ironically, it is also the film that, despite its reputation as the archetypal "arty" movie, caused Ono's avant-garde friends to drop her for being "too successful."

On May 19, 1968, the day after he called a meeting to tell the rest of the Beatles that he was Jesus Christ, Lennon invited Ono to his house, and the pair recorded the album that was to become *Unfinished Music No. 1: Two Virgins*, and then made love at dawn. That morning, Lennon's wife Cynthia came home to find Ono's slippers at the top of the stairs and, perhaps more revealingly, Ono herself, wearing Cynthia's dressing gown.

Ono began attending the sessions for the White Album, to the dismay of the rest of the band. She sang a line on "Bungalow Bill" and was the creative force behind "Revolution 9," the most experimental—and most divisive—piece of music ever to appear on a Beatles record. After a decade of having their wives and girlfriends patiently waiting in the background, the band suddenly found themselves with a Beatle whose partner wanted to be wherever her lover was whenever possible, and to be involved in every aspect of his career. During this time, Lennon wrote "Julia," the song whose chorus includes the English translation of Yoko's first name, "ocean child," and on August 22—the day that Ringo Starr walked out on the band—John and Cynthia Lennon were formally divorced.

Ono and Lennon's collaborative album *Two Virgins* was released in November. While its contents would have sounded familiar to anyone who had followed Ono's career, it was mystifying to Beatles fans, who until now had been faced with nothing weirder than some backward guitar and the odd confusing lyric. The album's nude cover alienated thousands of fans, many of whom had previously dreamed of seeing John Lennon in the nude, but had not bargained for him being accompanied by his new girlfriend, who was clearly a foreigner and a bit "artistic." The album's contents—avant-garde "noise" and spoken-word snippets—merely baffled the public, but the cover, which featured front and rear shots of Ono and Lennon in the nude, created an uproar. 30 years later, the album is still available, and is still the butt of a million jokes.

After 1968, and therefore after the period covered by this book, Ono and Lennon married. This led to some of the worst abuse any couple has ever experienced. The perception that

Ono "split up the Beatles" and the fact that she was a woman, and Japanese to boot, increased the fury. Things were worsened in the dull dead eyes of the press by Ono and Lennon's increased forays into the avant-garde as they attempted to publicize peace through their deliberately surreal "bed-in" campaigns. The press inevitably chose to misinterpret the humor of Ono/Lennon events, ignoring the fact that the participants also saw the ridiculousness of what they were doing. The most concrete result of this period, however—the single "Give Peace a Chance"—could not have existed without this well-meant and honest media collaboration between the pair.

Their relationship in the 1970s was a turbulent one. They even split up for a time, Lennon's "lost weekend" in Los Angeles being engendered by Ono's suggestion that he leave her. Their reunion, which resulted in the birth of their son, Sean Ono Lennon, and Lennon's commercial resurgence with the Ono/Lennon collaboration *Double Fantasy*, was overshadowed and mythologized by Lennon's murder in 1980. Ono suddenly found herself the most famous widow in the world and the curator of Lennon's legacy. From being hated as the Beatle-splitting Japanese woman, she has become John Lennon's respectable representative. Despite a rivalry between her and Paul McCartney (once described by Lennon as "an old estranged fiancée of mine"), Ono has looked after her former husband's legacy and reputation with dignity and restraint.

In 1968, however, the press and the public derided Lennon and Ono's relationship. Ono was seen as a Bad Influence, possibly using time travel to retrospectively supply the formerly lovable mop-top with drugs and long hair before they had even met. Her effect on Lennon was pretty immediate, too. Whereas Cynthia, unhappy but quiet, had always remained in the background, loving Lennon but unable to make him love her, part of Yoko's attraction for Lennon was her dynamic nature. She was a mysterious person who was given to making enigmatic public statements; a quiet person who made extreme art; an Asian woman with a sense of humor and a sense of her own importance as a woman and as an artist.

Lennon fell in love with Ono in a very public way. Part of him—the aggressive part—wanted to thrust her into the eyes of the public and of the other Beatles, defying them to tell her to go away. (In 1969, Harrison did virtually that, telling Ono that his New York friends had warned him about her.) The other part was simply overjoyed. Lennon wanted to make love to her, record albums with her, put on shows with her, go to bed with her in public, and introduce her to the Beatle world. (Her appearance with Lennon on the 1968 Beatles Christmas record, a flexidisc sent to all members of the Beatles Fan Club, now sounds charming—the in-jokey talk of a couple newly in love and all that—but at the time, it enraged several nations of fans.)

The great accusation leveled at Ono is that she split up the Beatles. This simplistic claim assumes that, before Yoko Ono came along, the Beatles were all getting along swimmingly, preparing to make album after album, happy and comfortable in their little Beatle world. And so, the story goes, after Ono appeared, her malign influence threw them into confusion and self-hatred, causing them to split up, record second-rate solo albums, bad movies, and, ultimately, write songs about Rupert the Bear and do voiceovers for Thomas the Tank Engine. This is patent nonsense. In 1968, the Beatles were, to a very large extent, about to go their own ways. Harrison was getting fed up with his role as the "third Beatle," both Lennon and McCartney were ending long relationships, and even Starr was finding new interests outside music. All the Beatles, not just Lennon, were exploring solo projects—McCartney less so, but then, the Beatles were fast becoming his project. The final nail in the coffin, the *Let It Be* fiasco, would have been a disaster even if Ono hadn't been sitting next to Lennon throughout the recording sessions. It's also worth noting that the last LP the Beatles actually recorded, *Abbey Road*, is a fine and shiny return to pop form, and Ono's influence—both musical and emotional—on Lennon's songs on that album is positive throughout. The solo careers of the various band members, too, were not disastrous. Away from the hypercritical Lennon and McCartney, Harrison suddenly found himself able to record *All Things Must Pass*, a fairly epic triple album that was a huge commercial and critical success all around the world. Starr, too, found his pop feet, and for a while was the most successful charting ex-Beatle (and his superb single "Photograph," co-written with Harrison, even suggests a world of Beatle pop that never happened).

The Beatle most affected by the split, Paul McCartney, suffered a huge crisis of confidence, which was sparked by the band's resentment of his attempts to keep them going and to stop them from hiring the goonish Allen Klein as manager. His early solo work is unfocused and shaky, lacking a Lennon both to write with and to edit his musical excesses. It took McCartney until 1973 to record his greatest solo album, *Band on the Run*; thereafter, his muse was intermittently brilliant, commercial, self-indulgent, and, at times, mawkish.

Lennon himself missed his partner's musicality from time to time, but the fact remains that his best solo work was done either in partnership with or under the influence of Ono. His first "musical" solo albums, *Plastic Ono Band* and *Imagine*, are peerless, and his last LP, *Double Fantasy*, while domestic and rosy in a way that McCartney at his worst could never be, was a melodic return to confidence. Separated from Ono, Lennon tended to record weak songs, bad pop statements, and the idea-less 1970s musician's fallback position, rock 'n' roll.

There's also the argument that it was Ono's career, not the Beatles', that suffered when she met Lennon. While the Fab Four went off in their various directions, Ono became stereotyped as "Mrs. Lennon" (a title she used for one of her own songs). Her art was always associated with Lennon, both as its sponsor and as its cocreator. She went into music, and Lennon's influence made sure that these albums, which, had they come out with little fanfare on small labels, might then have been judged for what they are—superior avant-garde rock—were instead recorded with Eric Clapton and session musicians, released on Apple, and forced to compete in the commercial mainstream. Just as Linda McCartney, with little or no musical background, found herself touring and recording with Wings, so Ono found herself promoted as a rock act. Not that she was averse to this. Even now, however, 20 years after the death of her husband, the best of her work—her recent *Bronze Age* exhibition, her superb *Rising* album—will always be judged as some kind of Beatles offshoot.

It would, admittedly, be either naive or crazy to say that Ono had no influence over this period of the Beatles' career. Lennon's insistence that she be everywhere he was caused friction. If McCartney had taken Linda Eastman with him to all the Beatle sessions, the same might have happened. A certain amount of wifely presence was acceptable—Patti Harrison and Maureen Starkey even sing backing vocals on the White Album—but Ono was there all the time, and while she was not the cause of the Beatles' decline, she certainly contributed to it, however unwittingly.

Barely two months after the sessions for the White Album ended, the Beatles found themselves in the cold and horrible Twickenham Studios to be filmed and recorded for the equally cold and horrible album *Let It Be*. Because the band was now playing together every day, the *Let It Be* sessions were even more negative than those of the White Album. There are unreleased tapes from this period, on which the Beatles discuss their then state of disarray and tension. McCartney is heard to say of Ono that he doesn't want her sitting on his amp. More tellingly, Linda McCartney says "Go away!" to an imaginary Yoko, and the film's director, Michael Douglas-Hogg, suggests that something might be put in Yoko's tea to knock her out so the Beatles can have a meeting as a foursome again. Both remarks are met with a silence that is not dissent.

Ultimately, however, the most important thing in Lennon's life was that he was with Ono, and 1968 and the White Album were the forum for the development of their relationship. One song on the White Album is evidence of this—"Julia," the song that is simultaneously a lament for Lennon's dead mother and a love song for Yoko Ono, "ocean child." It's a bridge between the two most important women in Lennon's life. He once explained his disillusionment with the Maharishi by saying that he was always looking for his mother, and never finding her. This time, it seemed that Lennon—who, later in his life, used "Mother" as a nickname for Ono—had finally filled a vacuum in his soul. Ono herself, lonely and isolated from her family and her artistic peers, with two failed marriages behind her, remained unimpressed by Lennon's pop fame, but deeply impressed by the sheer force of his personality. She was in love with someone who would love her for the rest of his life. The infighting and bitching of the Beatles was, and is, irrelevant compared to that.

THE PRODUCERS

The White Album is notable among Beatles records for being the first one that was not entirely produced by George Martin. The increasing tension within the band made a Beatles recording session an unpleasant place to be, and, for the first time, George Martin excused himself from some of the recording. This destabilized the sessions still further. Without Martin's supreme diplomacy and his presence as a kind of barrier between the sharp-tongued, arrogant Beatles and their long-suffering engineers (who would always be demonized by the forever-experimenting Beatles as people who only existed to block their exciting new ideas), the Beatles themselves become even more fractious and bad-tempered. The presence of more than one producer on a record is never a good sign, and in this case it explains not only much of the White Album's musical disunity, but also the wide range of production styles contained within it, from the delicacy of "Blackbird" to the constipated compression of "Savoy Truffle."

George Martin

From "Love Me Do" in 1962 to *Abbey Road* in 1969, from the hastily recorded *Please Please Me* album to the leisurely psychedelia of *Sgt. Pepper*, nearly every Beatles recording was produced by George Martin. Significantly, there are only two Beatles albums that are not notable for Martin's dry, clean sound. One is the career-ending, aptly black-sleeved gloomhole that is *Let It Be*, while the other is the sprawling White Album. While Martin did work on most of the White Album, he found much of the experience unpleasant, and even handed the album's last month of recording over to a fairly untested engineer, the young Chris Thomas.

George Martin's importance to the story of the Beatles is enormous. His personality—his old-school diplomacy and unflappability—belonged to a different era. Martin's almost stereotypically British background—wartime service as a lieutenant in the Fleet Air Arm, postwar work for the bureaucratic EMI empire—could easily have been just the kind of thing to annoy the early Beatles (particularly Lennon), but, as their relationship with Brian Epstein showed, they always warmed to authority figures who could advance their career. McCartney also pointed out the advantages of Martin's seemingly patrician background, referring to Martin's "excellent bedside manner" as the result of his military background: "He'd dealt with navigators and pilots...he could deal with us when we got out of line." Throughout the Beatles' recording career—wisely, he never impinged on any other aspect of their career—George Martin managed to handle and work effectively with three volatile individuals and Ringo Starr, steer them through their drug days, ignore their superstar fits, and, most important, translate their extraordinary ideas into reality. His pragmatism was always combined with a willingness to try something new. His ability with rock (he played the astonishing piano on McCartney's definitive version of "Long Tall Sally") gelled with his experience as a comedy producer—from *Yellow Submarine* to *Sgt. Pepper*, no 1960s producer used audio effects so well. His clean, focused productions gave the Beatles a cohesive, unique sound that, legend has it, caused producers around the world to rip up their studios in unsuccessful efforts to re-create it. On listening to even the least dramatic Beatles recording, one without backward tapes or sound effects or any of the distinctive trappings of the mid-1960s Beatle sound, Martin's production sounds clearer, louder, and more direct than almost any other recording of the era.

George Martin was born on January 3, 1926, in Holloway, North London. At school, he formed his own dance band. After school, he joined the Fleet Air Arm—the Royal Navy's airborne section—in 1943, and rose to the rank of lieutenant. After leaving the service, he went to work for Parlophone Records, a label that at the time was known largely for jazz and comedy records. As a result, Martin worked with an extraordinary variety of artists. Apart from his time in the classical section, he worked with everyone from British jazz couple Cleo Laine and John Dankworth, Humphrey Lyttelton, and Judy Garland to Peter Cook and Dudley Moore and the Goons, the anarchic radio comedy trio featuring future Beatle fan Peter Sellers, whose humor was such a huge influence on John Lennon's. In 1955, Martin became head of Parlophone Records.

On June 6, 1962, the Beatles came in to audition for Parlophone, having already been taken by Brian Epstein to, in Martin's own words, "every record label in the country." Martin had disliked the Beatles' demo tape—a ragbag of old R & B and novelty songs—but there was something about the band that appealed to him. "I fell in love with them," he said about his first meeting with the group. "I thought they were wonderful people."

Martin recognized their star quality, even though he thought they were nothing special as songwriters. (He later cited "Love Me Do," "P.S. I Love You," and "One After 909" as songs typical of their work at this time, so he has a point.) After a few rocky moments—George Harrison expressed dislike for Martin's tie, Martin replaced Ringo with session drummer Andy White on one version of "Love Me Do," and, most notably, Lennon rebelled over Martin's choice of "How Do You Do What You Do" as a single, insisting on "Please Please Me" instead—George Martin realized that he was dealing with "geniuses," and the relationship began in earnest.

Early Beatles productions were basic affairs—a chorus would be moved, a vocal would be double-tracked—but as the Beatles became more successful, the budgets increased, and so did the desire to experiment. After the thin-sounding, partly formulaic *Help!*, a change in approach was necessary. Beatles records started to contain a greater variety of instruments, new musical ideas, and a broader studio palette of effects and experimentation—all of which Martin either assisted with or introduced to the band (his speeded-up electric piano, doubling as a harpsichord, is a classic example of Martin at his most imaginative).

When the band was finally able to stop touring, it was at a time when their desire to do different things had escalated (along with their drug use). The band was excited by sonic experiment and introduced a new technique on seemingly every song. By the time *Revolver* was made, with its backward guitars, French horn solos, submarine sound effects, and tape loops, George Martin was forced to be much more than the chap who got the drums to sound nice. He was producing in the modern sense of the word, helping to create new sounds and inventing new ways of using sound.

He was more than keen to assist in the process, too. Martin dreamed of a fusion of all kinds of popular music, classical, rock, and pop. In the Beatles, he felt he had a band capable of doing this, with their use of string section-backed songs, sequential songwriting, and even themed pieces. All of these things came to a head on *Sgt. Pepper's Lonely Hearts Club Band*, an album that not only mixed up genres to an alarming extent (from pop and soul to acid rock, classical sitar to music hall) but also stretched Martin's technical imagination to the limits, whether he was gluing together streams of backward-playing steam organ tapes or hiring an orchestra to play one huge fat apocalyptic chord while wearing monster paw gloves.

Despite being the first Beatles album on which a Beatle went outside the band for assistance (McCartney enlisted Mike Leander to arrange "She's Leaving Home"), *Sgt. Pepper* was also the first album, in Martin's opinion, on which they had a proper amount of time to spend. He cites the lack of touring as the reason, but it's probably also true, given the revenue and success the Beatles were generating for EMI, that the label was, for once, happy to let the band effectively live in their workplace. By the time the White Album was made, recording sessions that lasted 12 hours were not uncommon. Six years before, whole albums might have been made in a day.

The Beatles may have been given a creative freedom available to no other band, and the making of *Sgt. Pepper* was without doubt their creative studio peak, but Martin would later claim that, as the band fell away from the pop arena and into a world of recording and rehearsing at will, they became undisciplined. He once went so far as to use the phrase "not enough mental discipline" to describe their work at this time, which is not, unfortunately, the kind of expression one hears from a lot of rock producers—just the ones who were lieutenants in the Fleet Air Arm in World War Two.

After the death of Brian Epstein and the rise of what bad social commentators always call the "let it all hang out" era, mental and others kinds of discipline were not so much frowned upon as pelted with rubbish and set alight in the town square. Rich, indulged, and hugely talented, the Beatles had always followed their instincts, and their instincts had made them the greatest band in the world. Now, able to do what they wanted and with no one to tell them what to do, the Beatles were about to find that their instincts were fallible.

After the *Magical Mystery Tour* EP, which saw Martin working at full capacity on the great "I Am the Walrus" and the rocking "Lady Madonna" (and perhaps less so on the hopeless "Your Mother Should Know") the next project was the ninth Beatles album. This was to be the first truly unpleasurable experience for Martin as a producer. Band tensions were running high, fights were frequent, and the atmosphere was legendarily unpleasant. On July 16, after less than two months recording, engineer Geoff Emerick resigned from the project. On August 22, Ringo Starr walked out. And on September 9, George Martin, the man most associated with the Beatles in the studio, decided to take a holiday in the middle of recording the new Beatles album. He didn't return until October 1, two weeks before recording ended. Martin would be absent even more during the recording of the next album, *Let It Be*, but the cracks were beginning to appear during the recording of the White Album.

Martin has always been famously ambivalent about the quality of the White Album. The first Beatles album on which he was not credited as sole producer, the White Album is also the first album where Martin wasn't particularly happy with the results.

The "single album" theory—the idea that the White Album should have been edited down from a rambling double to a concise, musically cohesive single—originated with Martin. This theory has led to a million compilation tapes of the album: they invariably omit "Revolution 9," genuinely inferior tracks such as "Wild Honey Pie," and agreeable duffers such as "Savoy Truffle" and "Don't Pass Me By." While this approach would have given the world a fantastic album, from "Back in the U.S.S.R." and "Happiness Is a Warm Gun" to "While My Guitar Gently Weeps" and "Blackbird," it would have denied listeners the extraordinary charms of "Cry Baby Cry," "Everybody's Got Something to Hide Except Me and My Monkey," "Long, Long, Long," and the super-but-often-reviled "Revolution 9." Having not enough great songs for a double album can also translate as having too many great songs for a single album. Then again, how much better would *Let It Be* have been with the odd bit of leftover White Album on it?

Martin—who also believed that the album was so long because the band wanted to get out of its EMI contract faster, wrongly believing that a double album counted as two releases rather than one—has not greatly changed his views on the White Album over the years. In 1971 he told the press that the White Album was excellent, but too long, and he does not seem to have altered his position greatly since that time. "It was a marvelous album, but it was up and down," he told one Internet journalist recently. "There were some great ones, and there were some not so great ones." (Tact and manners have always been Sir George's forte.) He also added, perceptively, that after Brian Epstein's death, the Beatles "tended to go off in their own directions" and concludes, with admirable succinctness, "They brought me a whole host of songs, all of which they wanted to record." And, he does not have to add, all of which they did record. And release.

It was a difficult album for Martin to record. Tensions aside, the band members were working as solo entities to such an extent that they would often be working individually in two or three different studios at the same time. (Harrison claims this was because they were up against a release deadline.) Martin has recalled that he had to "split myself three ways," and that the whole process of making the album became "very fragmented." He has expressed dissatisfaction with the album's lack of unity. After *Sgt. Pepper*, which gives the perfect illusion of a themed, sequenced piece of rock music, Martin felt that the White Album was just a collection of songs by John, Paul, and George as individuals, and thus was effectively a step back for the band as a unit. Since the 1960s, of course, the efforts of various bands, most notably the progressive rock acts of the 1970s, to make concept albums (and in doing so, bore the ears off millions), have put the idea of the themed album into disrepute. In 1968, however, it really did seem like a way forward for rock, which was still hankering after some kind of maturity and adult acceptability. Similarly, albums such as *Revolver* and *Rubber Soul*, which are celebrated today specifically for their diversity of songs and for the different styles of their three songwriters, were at the time seen as nothing more than pop albums—great pop albums, admittedly, but the reverence they have accumulated in recent years was a long way off.

George Martin had enjoyed producing *Sgt. Pepper*, most significantly the process of "piecing it together and cutting in sound effects and so on." "I thought this was a good thing, and I was rather sad when we did the White Album that we'd chucked that out of the window," he said later. (Martin was eventually able to get his way again with the seemingly unified and beautifully sequenced *Abbey Road*, an album that in many ways is a glossy, more "adult" *Sgt. Pepper*.)

Martin is not merely a producer who loves cozy pop tunes. Despite his leanings toward conciseness and great songs, he is a fan of the most extreme Beatles' track, "Revolution 9." He supplied Lennon with the phrase "Happiness Is a Warm Gun," which was taken from a weapons magazine he had once seen. And the best of the White Album is informed by that clear George Martin sound, at once deep and sharp and, like its creator, never fussy and never vague. Even despite his occasional absences, the White Album is a superb George Martin sound production, and it owes much of its quality to Martin's brilliance as a producer.

After the Beatles split, the cooling-off of the White Album and the hell of *Let It Be* took its toll on Martin's relationship with his former protégés. John Lennon, with his usual charm, once remarked, "Show me a tune that George Martin's written," while Martin himself compared his Fab-free new life to having lots of one-night stands after having been married. He has, since those unhappy times, worked with Paul McCartney several times, most notably (in terms of excellence) on the orchestral, dramatic theme song for the James Bond movie *Live and Let Die*. In 2001, he became one of the few British producers ever to have his work commemorated in a boxed set. He is almost certainly the only British rock producer ever to be knighted—an award he got before Paul McCartney, which is only right and proper.

Chris Thomas

Chris Thomas is one of the most important producers in British rock music. He has worked with the best British bands of each era, from Pink Floyd (on *Dark Side of the Moon*) and Roxy Music to the Sex Pistols, the Pretenders, and, in the 1990s, Pulp. Thomas's sound is a distinctive one. Chunky, loud, and clear, it forms a direct musical link all the way from the Sex Pistols' "Anarchy in the U.K." to Pulp's "Common People."

Chris Thomas began his musical career as a child, studying the violin and the piano at the Royal Academy of Music. Like most of the western world, a chance hearing of "Love Me Do" on Radio Luxembourg sent him into the evil arms of rock music, and he became a musician in London. After turning down the chance to join the Jimi Hendrix Experience as a bass player (no, really) at the age of 21, Thomas decided he wanted to be a producer. "I didn't want to fiddle around working my way to the top. I wanted to do it straight away," he said many years later, which probably explains why, after a couple of false starts, he went to the top to get a job in the form of asking George Martin for work. Martin arranged an interview for Thomas that lead to him working at Martin's AIR Studios on six months' trial. "That was obviously tea-boy, messenger boy, anything that was around to do," he recalled later. "Basically they said, 'Hang around. Come down to any session you like.'"   ·

After a couple of months at AIR, Thomas asked Martin, with some powerful casualness, if he could come down to the sessions for the White Album. Martin said yes, and Thomas "sat in the corner for a couple of months" while the band recorded. Thomas described the situation, he with his youth and inexperience, the Beatles with their world-famousness, as "ridiculous." Things became more ridiculous three months later when George Martin decided to go on holiday. "I had just come back from holiday myself," said Thomas later, "and when I came in there was a little letter on the desk that said, 'Dear Chris, Hope you had a nice holiday. I'm off on mine now. Make yourself available to the Beatles. Neil [Aspinall] and Mal [Evans] know you're coming down.'"

Chris Thomas was 22. The Beatles' engineer, Ken Scott, was 21. And they were working with the most famous band in the world (who were in their late 20s, pushing 30).

Things went from weird to worse. After hearing Lennon say to someone, "He's not really doing his job, is he?" and assuming Lennon meant him, Thomas decided he was about to be sacked. This impression was strengthened later when, from up in the control room during a recording session, he interrupted the band's playing to tell them they had made a mistake and should try again. Fortunately for the young Thomas, the Beatles agreed.

After that, Thomas's career failed to end. He worked on "Happiness Is a Warm Gun," played harpsichord on "Piggies" (he now claims that, as he couldn't play in time, his playing was never used) and played Mellotron on "Bungalow Bill" live in the studio with the Beatles. It was a baptism-by-fire for Thomas, even down to working in different studios with different Beatles as the deadline for the White Album neared. Thomas's post-Beatles career (which has included more work with McCartney) has always reflected its endurance-test genesis.

Geoff Emerick

Geoff Emerick worked extensively with the Beatles, and since that time has gone on to become a successful and popular producer. His first job with the Beatles was to assist George Martin on, of all things, the backing tracks for "Tomorrow Never Knows." Beatle trivia fans treasure Geoff Emerick always, because he smoked the brand of cigarettes—Everest—that nearly provided the name of the last Beatles album, *Let It Be*. He went on to work with everyone from Echo and the Bunnymen to Elvis Costello, and provided a valuable link between Elvis Costello and Paul McCartney when they collaborated in the 1980s. He was also the first person to walk out on the White Album's sessions. No one has ever suggested he did the wrong thing.

Ken Scott

Scott was a youthful 21 when he worked as an engineer on the White Album. He went on to be better known for his work with David Bowie in the early 1970s. Bowie once referred to Scott as his "George Martin." Mad trivia fans who seek a stronger link between David Bowie and the Beatles will be delighted to learn that the piano used on Bowie's *The Rise and Fall of Ziggy Stardust and the Spiders from Mars* album is the same piano that was played during the original recording of "Hey Jude." Ken Scott has since gone on to work with George Harrison, Supertramp, Devo, and, perhaps most notably, the Mahavishnu Orchestra on its album *Emerald Visions of the Pure Beyond*.

the songs

"I think it's the best music we've made. But as a Beatles
thing, as a whole, it doesn't work."

John Lennon

THE WHITE ALBUM WAS RELEASED ON NOVEMBER 22, 1968, in
the United Kingdom, and three days later in the United
States. Both sets of pressings initially featured serial numbers,
American ones differing by the one letter A prefix (although
there was much duplication of serial numbers, as, for
example, each of the 12 U.K. pressing plants numbered their
records from 1 upwards, so there are 12 number ones, and so
forth). American copies had white inner sleeves, as opposed
to black ones in the United Kingdom, and the four photos
inside were smaller. Rumor has it that Capitol, the Beatles'
U.S. label, tried to alter the sound of the album by com-
pressing it, but was stopped by George Harrison.

The Beatles, as it was officially known, was the first Beatles
album to be released on the band's new Apple label. There are
no contemporary singles from the album (although both "Back
in the U.S.S.R." and "Ob-La-Di, Ob-La-Da" came out as 45s in
1976). The White Album, as the record soon came to be
known, was the first Beatles album to be largely demoed—that
is, to have its songs "tried out" by recording them in rough
form on tape in advance of their studio recording. The Beatles
all met at the end of May 1968 to play their new songs to each
other at George Harrison's house, Kinfauns, in Esher, Surrey.
This situation arose partly because the band had written so

many new songs while at Rishikesh, the Maharishi Mahesh Yogi's retreat in India, and partly because they were no longer collaborating at all on songs, and were now used to working independently on their own material.

The Kinfauns demos have, inevitably, surfaced on various bootlegs—illegally made recordings sold without the artist's permission. The Kinfauns tapes and other bootlegs (the Beatles must be the most bootlegged band of all time) are deeply illegal and financially immoral items. They are, however, intriguing glimpses into the band's songwriting methods and the way the Beatles put together the White Album.

The Beatles all liked the White Album. John Lennon called it a collection of solo recordings, claiming—with some justification—that it was "me and a backing group, Paul and a backing group." Paul McCartney, always the band's most consistent and melodic writer, had some of his best songs on the White Album. George Harrison liked side one best, and had his largest ever total of songs—four—on the album. Ringo Starr felt it was a better collection of songs than *Sgt. Pepper*, and it included his first ever solo composition.

In the wake of its predecessor, *Sgt. Pepper*, the White Album's release was anticipated by millions. Despite the fact that it was a double album and was therefore expensive—it cost 73 shillings at the time (£3.65, or roughly $5), advance sales of the White Album reached 300,000 in Britain and 1,900,000 in the United States. By the end of 1968, it had sold an astonishing four million copies; not bad for an album that had come out at the end of November. (Until the release of the *Saturday Night Fever* soundtrack a decade later, the White Album was the best-selling double album of all time.)

It was followed within weeks by the release of *Yellow Submarine*, an animated cartoon featuring an out-of-date version of the Beatles and some strange songs from 1967. Twelve weeks after completing the sessions for the White Album, the Beatles were recording again, this time in the frosty caves of Twickenham Studios. The results of these sessions—intended by McCartney to revitalize the band— were a grim but riveting documentary and a grim but sometimes powerful album. After the hell of recording *Let It Be*, the band went into the studios with George Martin, recorded the slick *Abbey Road*, allowed *Let It Be* to come out, and split up, exhausted and litigious.

SIDE ONE

Back in the U.S.S.R.

(Credit: Lennon/McCartney. Actual writer: Paul McCartney, with some input from Mike Love)

The White Album could not have a more promising start—the screaming roar of a jet engine taking off, an excited chord, and one of the best barnstorming rock riffs of the 1960s, all leading into Paul McCartney's most powerful rocker. "Back in the U.S.S.R." is ironic (in its use of Beach Boys melody and metaphor), funny (in its subject matter), and, more important, exciting. It thunders along like the jet airliner it mimics, takes corners at incredible speed, and is stuffed full of musical puns. It is one of the Beatles' greatest songs, and is widely regarded as the best rock song they ever wrote (they were always more at ease rocking out on their versions of Chuck Berry and Little Richard songs). "Back in the U.S.S.R." was so popular that in the mid-1970s it earned the dubious tribute of becoming a posthumous single when it was released to promote the Beatles' *Rock 'n' Roll Music* compilation. (The nation failed to buy it, realizing perhaps that a single of "Back in the U.S.S.R." was in some way a kind of cheating.)

Paul McCartney has always been a master of pastiche and parody. From soul tunes such as "Got to Get You Into My Life" to music-hall songs such as "When I'm 64," he has maintained an almost glib facility for diverse musical styles. The other Beatles never seemed too bothered by this sort of thing: Lennon probably regarded it as party-trick cleverness, and Harrison was too busy trying not to rewrite other people's stuff. Certainly this kind of dexterity can come across as too clever by half (one thinks of the French lyrics in "Michelle" and asks, why, Lord, why?), but when McCartney is on, he's on. In lesser, feebler, hands, "Back in the U.S.S.R." could have been a rotten comedy song, a weak parody tune, but McCartney—cocky, confident, and able to do almost anything musically—made it into something amazing.

The song's title crams in all sorts of contemporary and less-contemporary allusions. It apparently started as a reference to a bizarre pro-UK government campaign called "I'm Backing Britain." Just how one was supposed to back Britain was never made clear, but the slogan, in those more innocent days, was quite popular. From "I'm Backing Britain" came thoughts of Chuck Berry's song "Back in the U.S.A." Chuck Berry was one of the Beatles' favorite songwriters, and his work had influenced them in many ways before. McCartney's "I'm Down," for example, is a not-so-distant cousin of Berry's "Too Much Monkey Business." "Back in the

U.S.A." is one of Berry's most cheerful songs, a wild and leaping tribute to the country that only months before had jailed him. It was no surprise that one of his titles would be floating in the Beatles' ether, especially when that ether was one of the most pun-filled atmospheres in pop.

McCartney's sense of humor—a quality that is always underrated in pop and rock, in which suicidal determination and hard-faced romanticism are more popular than the ability to find things ridiculous—kicked in at this point to make the song's gripping twist. This was to be a rock 'n' roll song glorifying not the sunkissed beaches and cantilevered bikinis of America, but the freezing wastes and iron totalitarianism of the Soviet Union, which was Not A Fun Place At All.

Only a British person, or at least a non-American, could have written a song on this theme at the time. Years of Cold War and actual war with, respectively, the Soviet Union and her satellites and allies, had made America fairly certain that the Russians were not fit subjects for affectionate joshing. But in Britain, where the streets were filled with communists and where the Red Menace was viewed with slightly less alarm than the threat from plaid-panted American tourists called Hiram thronging the streets of London and mispronouncing Worcestershire (it's "Wooster-sher,") there was something funny about the U.S.S.R. The song's concept was novel, too. Writing a song about how sexy Russia might be was a new idea, as good as anything anyone writing books or making movies might come up with.

The third element of McCartney's brilliance was making the song not a Chuck Berry number—which would be so obvious and ordinary that it probably never even occurred to

McCartney to try it—but a Beach Boys pastiche. The Beach Boys were a big band in the 1960s, one of the biggest in the world. Insofar as pop went (as opposed to rock) they were the only rivals to the Beatles. McCartney and chief Beach Boys writer Brian Wilson had even had a brief period of musical rivalry around the mid-1960s. Albums such as *Rubber Soul*, *Pet Sounds*, and *Revolver* all reflected back on each other as Wilson and McCartney (as well as Lennon) discovered they could broaden their musical range and write songs that, lyrically and musically, went everywhere.

Sadly, while the Beatles' route took them into newer and more exciting regions that were rewarding both spiritually and commercially, Brian Wilson's efforts were shouted down by drug use. The most exciting American composer of the 1960s all but lost his mind completely from LSD consumption. (He was also brought down to a lesser extent by his band's and his record label's furious insistence that, essentially, he stop writing wistful, noodling songs about his emotions and hammer out a load of stuff about surfboards and sex.)

By 1968, the Beach Boys were no longer rivals to the Beatles, but when the Fab Four discovered the Maharishi Mahesh Yogi and his teachings, they were joined in India by Mike Love, Beach Boy and composer of "California Girls." Love was, ironically, the chief instigator of the campaign to make the Beach Boys unimaginative and more popular again. A life-and-soul-of-the-party type of fellow, he was described by at least one other Rishikesh visitor as "someone I didn't take to." Against this impression is the fact that Mike Love was a keen follower of the Maharishi's teachings, and even entitled a Beach Boys' song "T. M. Song." He still practices the disciplines he learned in the 1960s. Out in Rishikesh, the Beatles and Love became meditation buddies, and when it turned out that Love would be celebrating his birthday while in Rishikesh, the Beatles wrote a song for him, called, naturally given the circumstances, "Spiritual Regeneration."

"Spiritual Regeneration" is a slight thing, the band playing acoustics and messing around. Being a Beatles song, however, it's also a work of brilliance. Over thrumming acoustic chords, Lennon and McCartney sing about the wonderfulness of Guru Dev and so forth, but they do so to a near-perfect pastiche of the Beach Boys' "Surfin' U.S.A." The result is hilarious, a surf tune about spiritual regeneration, with Beach Boy-close harmonies (Lennon on falsetto and McCartney on bass vocals) behind religious lyrics. It's also very charming, especially when, after a brief talkover section explaining that the song is for Mike Love's birthday, the song mutates into "Happy Birthday Mike Love." Both as a musical pastiche and as a reminder of the times when life at Rishikesh was an innocent and hopeful affair, "Spiritual Regeneration" is a fascinating piece of music. It also acts as a very clear indication that the Beach Boys and their music were very much in Paul McCartney's mind in early 1968. It's no surprise that "Back in the U.S.S.R." was one of the songs ready to be demoed at Kinfauns that May. (It's also no surprise that Mike Love claims to have had some influence over the song's lyrics, saying that he recommended frequent mention of girls in the lyric. Certainly the song parodies the lyric for "California Girls" in its list of regional Soviet female types.) Many years later, when he had come out of the terrible fog of depression and mental illness that consumed him for decades, Brian Wilson said of "Back in the U.S.S.R.," "I didn't even recognize that until someone said something. I thought that was really adorable."

Recorded by the Beatles some three months after the demo, "Back in the U.S.S.R." was pretty much ready when McCartney took it into Abbey Road. The Kinfauns demo is a little slower and, by virtue of being played on acoustic guitar, somewhat basic. The final verse—the one about "snow-peaked mountains"—is absent (and on the first verse, McCartney sings "awful flight" instead of the snappier "dreadful flight.") But harmonies and chorus are already present, as are the song's gently acerbic lyrics about phone-tapping, sickbags, and, a great pun hitting a great song title, having "Georgia on my mind".

The song should have been easy to record. Lennon always enjoyed playing on rockers, and the band had never been sulky when presented with a song as good as this one. But these were changing times, and McCartney—prefiguring his unwitting heavy-handedness during the *Let It Be* sessions—decided to criticize Starr's drum playing, apparently objecting to a poorly executed tom-tom roll. Under pressure from the tensions in the studio, the fights, and the confusing presence of Yoko Ono, Starr, not an argumentative man, opted to walk out of the session rather than fight his corner.

The rest of the Beatles, perhaps placing creativity above sympathy, carried on with the session. McCartney played drums himself and the results are excellent, if slightly less Beatley. Lennon and Harrison (and McCartney) play superb guitar throughout, and the harmonies are hilarious. The whole thing rocks—and rocks substantially more than the Beach Boys ever did.

Recorded August 22 at Abbey Road. Overdubbed August 23.

Paul McCartney: lead vocals, drums, guitar, piano, lead guitar, backing vocals
John Lennon: lead guitar, bass, backing vocals
George Harrison: lead guitar, backing vocals
Ringo Starr: absent in a huff

Dear Prudence

(Credit: Lennon/McCartney. Actual writer: John Lennon)

The Beatles' stay in Rishikesh was pivotal to the White Album for several reasons. Not least among these were the time it gave the band to write new songs, away from the drugs and gadgetry of London, and the sense they had there of living in the now and being part of a community, which also imparted itself to their songs. Songs such as "Mother Nature's Son," Lennon's "Child of Nature," and "Dear Prudence" could not have been written if the band had not spent time in a small, intimate, and isolated group of people. The more negative flipside of this experience was to come soon enough, but for a short, innocent period, Rishikesh gave the Beatles a chance to step outside their small world of pop star life.

Writing songs based on personal experience had not always played a big part in Beatle compositional processes. The earliest Lennon and McCartney lyrics were just different ways of combining the words "I," "love," and "you," hence their excitement at subverting that lyrical form by writing "She Loves You," which at the time was a breakthrough for them. Later they began to tap into personal experience—from Lennon's coded description of an affair in "Norwegian

Wood" to the skewed acid nostalgia of "Penny Lane" and "Strawberry Fields Forever"—but LSD and the isolated life of the megastar meant that Beatles songs were rarely outward-looking. In Rishikesh, Lennon in particular found himself writing "reportage" songs, lyrics that reflected what was happening around him in almost literal detail. This was the new way of seeing that would inform songs like "Revolution" and his later work. Lennon was still searching his soul, but he was also engaging with the outside world as he did so.

"Dear Prudence," written in Rishikesh, is one of the most literal songs of all time. The lyric is an entreaty to a girl called Prudence, begging her to come outside and greet the new day. This is because it's what the song was designed to do. Prudence is Prudence Farrow, the sister of the actress and famous-person-marrier Mia Farrow. Prudence had apparently (and somewhat vaguely) "meditated too much," and would not come out of her chalet. Lennon and Harrison were sent to coax her out, and this song was part of the process.

The Rishikesh attendees were not, to say the least, the classic 1960s hippies of legend, sitting 'round in cheap teepees and rolling their own cigarettes to save money, but the alternative wing of the rich and famous. In Rishikesh there were TV actors, and pop stars such as Mike Love and Donovan, and the Farrow sisters themselves were not exactly the normal kind of hippie traveler. Their mother was Maureen O'Sullivan, who had played Jane in the Tarzan movies. Their father was the writer and director John Farrow. (John and Maureen married, brilliantly, during the filming of *Tarzan Escapes*.) The Farrows had heard of the Maharishi through the Beatles, and Mia was present partly as therapy after her divorce from Frank Sinatra. These days she continues to act, after her acrimonious separation from Woody Allen, while Prudence Farrow is a film producer based in Florida whose best-known movie is the thriller *Widow's Peak*.

Wealthy weekend hippies or not, the Rishikesh community was a real one, and their beliefs were sincere. Even John Lennon thought that enlightenment was just around the corner. The loss of this belief is almost certainly why, when he came to demo "Dear Prudence," there was a distinct note of cynicism in his presentation. Toward the end of the original tape, Lennon adds an acerbic talk-over section. Laughing, he claims that Farrow went "completely berserk under the care of Maharishi Mahesh." He further alleges that "all the people around her were very worried because she was going completely insane." Recording his demo after the alleged sexual assault incident—on the original tape, the song is followed by its damning flipside, "Sexy Sadie"— Lennon chose to interpret events in an anti-Maharishi light. At the time, it's possible that Farrow—who had only turned 20 a few weeks before flying to Rishikesh—had indeed overindulged in meditation and gone "slightly barmy," to use Lennon's phrase.

By the time "Dear Prudence" was recorded, Rishikesh was some months in the past, and the song was quite divorced from its original purpose. Now its strange title could be taken as almost Victorian-sounding, and its lyric an invitation to tune in or drop out. In fact, it is one of the band's spookiest recordings, almost a companion piece to "Cry Baby Cry" or Harrison's "Long, Long, Long," and one of the songs that would have best suited the album's original title, *A Doll's House*.

John Lennon's acid eeriness was still in the air at this point, and the style of spooky songwriting he'd kicked off on *Revolver* (and would soon reject for the simplistic rock of his early solo work) reached its peak on the White Album and, arguably, this song. Lennon's wide-eyed vocals, the breathy harmonies, and the spiraling guitar riff make "Dear Prudence" an almost ghostly song of exhortation. This ambience—so at odds with the floaty hippie vibe of India—goes a long way toward explaining why the 1980s punk/psychedelic/Goth band Siouxsie and the Banshees were able to cover the song so successfully, bringing out its buried but implicit sun-blinded sense of menace.

In recording terms, "Dear Prudence" also hints at the division among the Beatles. Having walked out a few days before, Ringo Starr did not play on this track (thus making him absent from the first two songs on the album), and was replaced by a slightly clompy but effective McCartney. The somewhat Ringo-ish backing vocals—the deep, nasal "look around 'round 'round"s—are provided, not by Starr, but by Beatles roadie and gopher Mal Evans, McCartney's cousin John, and Apple Records recording artist Jackie Lomax. (Lomax would soon record Harrison's "Sour Milk Sea," another Kinfauns demo.)

Recorded August 28 at Trident Studios. Overdubbed August 29 and 30.

John Lennon: lead vocals, guitar, backing vocals
Paul McCartney: bass, drums, piano, flugelhorn, backing vocals
George Harrison: lead guitar, backing vocals
Ringo Starr: absent

Glass Onion

(Credit: Lennon/McCartney. Actual writer: John Lennon)

Once again, the Beatles go for the solar plexus. This song's punch is not so much musical—although it does clatter along fantastically on McCartney's rattling bass—as it is lyrical. John Lennon's vocal is part tease, part taunt, and an all-out assault on the innocent Beatle fan, sitting at home, headphones on, lyric sheet on lap, desperately trying to work out what these songs all mean. And for John Lennon, there could have been no better way to subvert that fanaticism than to write a song that gets a rise out of the listener. On the surface, "Glass Onion" seems like a code-breaker's key, a Rosetta Stone for the Beatles' lyrical secrets. In fact, it's what Lennon would have called a "piss-take," a cruel mockery of all that the superfan loves the most. On the White Album, Lennon targets several groups in his satirical way—white hunters, gold diggers, gun users—but on this track, his target is the fans.

Lennon's overriding obsession, brought on, perhaps, after years of being "grinning Beatle John," was honesty. In his eyes, he had started in the Beatles as a leather-jacketed rocker, and had been made to dress up in a nice suit to become famous and acceptable. Once established as a lovable mop top, he had been told to keep quiet about his marriage to Cynthia, and then, as that marriage soured, he found he had to keep up the facade of devoted husband and dad. When he met and fell in love with Yoko Ono, he was able to dump the hypocrisy of both his marriage and his position as Popular Entertainer Number One. Freed from these responsibilities, Lennon was now able to say what he wanted to, and increasingly he did just that.

Being John Lennon, however, he wasn't always going to be direct about things. In fact, he described this song as him "having a laugh." And so "Glass Onion," the only song on the White Album that harks back musically to the Beatles' psychedelic era, would not be a terrifically blunt affair where Lennon basically harangued Beatles fans and told them to get over it. (This would be saved for "God," the "dream is over" climax to his solo album *John Lennon/Plastic Ono Band*.) Instead, "Glass Onion" is a "do you get it?" mocking tune in which Lennon scatters imaginary clues to a nonexistent riddle all over the place and invites us all to make fools of ourselves trying to work it out. The answer, if there is one (which there isn't, "Glass Onion" being a very 1960s song in that respect), is in the title. "Glass Onion" is an extremely aptly-named song. Peel away the layers of an onion and there is, of course, nothing there (try it at home, it's great), but with a glass onion, you don't even have to peel. The essential nothingness of it is on display for all to see.

The song takes the form of a riddle session. Lennon name-drops a lot of Beatles songs, mostly fairly recent ones. He informs us that he told us about Strawberry Fields, that he told us about the Walrus and that he told us about the Fool on the Hill. He makes references to "Lady Madonna" and "fixing a hole," and claims that the Walrus was, in fact, Paul (McCartney). The whole thing is the world's first post-modern self-referential rock song, an answer record to a question no one but the most fanatical, maddest Beatles fans would have asked.

Lennon may have got the idea from McCartney's "Lady Madonna," which itself quotes "I Am the Walrus" (and "Glass

Onion" almost certainly gave Harrison the idea of referring to, of all things, "Ob-La-Di, Ob-La-Da" in "Savoy Truffle"— wow, heavy), but he took it in his own direction. The allusion to "Fixing a Hole" takes the twist of trying to fix a hole in the ocean—that is to say, doing something pointless. Meanwhile, just to rub it in, the announcement that there's a fool on a hill who's still there is probably a dig at the listener.

The song's most famous claim—that Paul was the walrus—was something Lennon was keen to explain at the time. He said the gesture was partially a reference to the fact that, in the *Magical Mystery Tour* movie, McCartney was the member of the band who wore the walrus costume. Lennon also claimed he had written the line as a way of "throwing a crumb" (of praise) to McCartney for his work in keeping the band together (although it could just as easily have been for quoting "I Am the Walrus" in "Lady Madonna"). This is a deeply patronizing action, even from a man who at the time was engaged in the process of ending his relationship with Paul McCartney.

If the song was meant to stop Beatles fans from looking for meaning in the songs, it failed. Several latched onto the walrus/Paul reference and pointed out that, in some cultures, a walrus is an image of death. (What isn't, somewhere?) Most, however, found the song sexy and baffling. It certainly contains some of Lennon's best imagery, in the vein of "Happiness Is a Warm Gun." Where that song uses its images to create menace, however, Lennon's references to bent-backed tulips and cast iron shore (the Liverpool nickname of a particularly nasty stretch of beach by the River Mersey) add no extra layers to "Glass Onion."

Another rendition of the song exists, weirdly, in a fake mix done by bootleggers. There is also an early mix by Lennon, lacking George Martin's very 1967 strings (which bow us out of the song wonderfully and then get a hammering from Lennon's opening chords to "Ob-La-Di, Ob-La-Da"). This early mix ends, for no particular good reason other than spontaneity and fun, with the looped voice of a football commentator shouting, "It's a goal!"

Recorded September 11, 12, and 13 and October 10 at Abbey Road.

John Lennon: lead vocals, acoustic guitar
Paul McCartney: bass, piano, recorder
George Harrison: lead guitar
Ringo Starr: drums
Orchestra

Ob-La-Di, Ob-La-Da

(Credit: Lennon/McCartney. Actual writer: Paul McCartney with Jimmy Scott)

No one ever accused Paul McCartney of peddling doom and disaster, and on "Ob-La-Di, Ob-La-Da," he demonstrates why this is. "Ob-La-Di, Ob-La-Da" is the jauntiest song in the Beatles' entire catalog (and may even be McCartney's perkiest tune, which is saying something). Its mood of casual optimism, its hummable tune and utterly indestructible chorus, which remains lodged in the skull long after the actual brain has turned to dust and been scattered by the wind, are all classic Paul McCartney. At his worst, McCartney is the man who wrote "Wonderful

Christmastime" and "We All Stand Together." At his best, however, he is an optimistic, melodic, and original writer who can actually make the listener want to be more alive more often. This is a rare skill, especially in rock music, where songwriters put a couple of minor chords into a song and think they are the new Mahler. And "Ob-La-Di, Ob-La-Da"—jaunty or not—is a fantastic song. If you don't like "Ob-La-Di, Ob-La-Da," you are an enemy of pleasure, melody, and humanity. Be careful, non-lovers of "Ob-La-Di, Ob-La-Da:" you may be Lou Reed.

You may also be one of the Beatles, because they hated "Ob-La-Di, Ob-La-Da." At this point in their career, the Beatles became more and more concerned with writing songs for themselves as individuals rather than for a band. McCartney was especially concerned with "getting it right." He tended to come in with an idea of exactly how he wanted a song to sound. This not only created friction within the rest of the band—it implied that their contributions were at worst, irrelevant, and at best, could be duplicated by someone else— but also led to McCartney demanding retake after retake of his songs. Even John Lennon, a man who surely never had any problems getting his own way, was heard to remark that the Beatles would work for hours on one of Paul's songs and then knock off one of the others' tunes if there was time. (This would lead to George Harrison's final dissatisfaction with McCartney during the *Let It Be* sessions.)

The fact that the songs McCartney always wanted to work on the most were the jaunty ones cannot have helped, either. (Famously, he drove the rest of the Beatles to distraction with his obsessive reworkings of "Maxwell's Silver

Hammer," a song whose charm fades rapidly—and must have been a boiling hell to actually have to rehearse again and again.) "Ob-La-Di, Ob-La-Da" was one of those songs, as McCartney led the rest of the band through its chirpy choruses again and again and again (which is probably why Lennon's falsetto "thank you!" at the end of the recording sounds so heartfelt).

It's hard to imagine now what sound McCartney had in mind when he first wrote the song, but there are clues. First, the song is in what broadsheet music journalists would call "the ska idiom," i.e., it has a ska beat. Ska, also known in the United Kingdom as bluebeat, after the Jamaican record company of the same name, is a West Indian variant on soul music whose differentiating characteristic is a massive emphasis on the offbeat. This gives the music a bouncy, immensely likeable quality. Ska first hit the United Kingdom in the mid-1960s via Millie's "My Boy Lollipop"—an atom bomb of a single. By the end of the decade, just before it mutated into reggae, ska was immensely popular: its bizarre, local-referencing lyrics, sense of humor, and ineffably danceable beat made it a favorite of the immigrant community, teenagers, young children, and, somewhat para-doxically, violent racist skinheads alike. (If you'd like to know more about ska, there's a particularly good episode of *Police Squad* where Johnny the Snitch explains it to Dick Clarke.)

Early versions of "Ob-La-Di, Ob-La-Da," recorded at Kinfauns and Abbey Road, are arranged differently from the album version. The song's beat is carried on massed acoustic guitars that not only take it away from its Jamaican rhythmic origins, but also muffle and slow down the pace of the tune.

The song's innate liveliness still shines through, but it seems to be wrapped in cotton wool. Frustrated, McCartney could not make "Ob-La-Di, Ob-La-Da" into the up tune he wanted it to be. The other Beatles became equally frustrated as sessions plodded on. Ironically and predictably, it was Lennon who intervened and saved "Ob-La-Di, Ob-La-Da." Annoyed with the song to the point of near-fury, he hammered out an intro on a studio piano and insisted quite loudly that this was the way to do the song. And, as it turns out, Lennon was right. The new, piano-driven version of "Ob-La-Di, Ob-La-Da" has a vigor that the others lacked. This time around, McCartney's slightly complacent lyrics are not matched by a reassuring musical canter, but rather by Lennon's enraged gallop on the ivories. It is, in short, a classic Beatles moment, the coziness of Paul McCartney upended by the aggression of John Lennon.

"Ob-La-Di, Ob-La-Da" may be a superb pop tune, and—thanks to the popular 1970s "Blue" compilation—in the mind of millions was actually a hit single, but at the time the band didn't release it as a single. This is largely because the rest of the Beatles were heartily sick of the song and never wanted to hear it again. Unfortunately for them, the Scottish beat group Marmalade seized the moment and had their biggest ever hit single, thus ensuring that the single most famous song from the White Album at the time was also the one that most of the band itself could not stand.

Thematically, this song fits into another McCartney bag that the other Beatles found annoying—the "character" song. This was, and is, a whole strand in British pop music, associated for some reason with a peculiarly English kind of song. It has been a major feature of the work of several artistes and bands associated with the idea of Englishness: the Kinks, Ian Dury, Madness, and Blur have all, in various ironic and non-ironic ways, continued the tradition. The whole British suburban tradition—the unusual life lived behind net curtains—informs this kind of songwriting. And one of its greatest exponents was, and is, Paul McCartney. From "Eleanor Rigby" and "Paperback Writer" to "Lovely Rita" and "She's Leaving Home," Paul McCartney was deeply fond of writing songs that served as little vignettes of the lives of imaginary people. John Lennon tended to avoid this sort of thing, and he was usually sniffy about it when McCartney did it (for an exception, see the entry on "The Continuing Story of Bungalow Bill"). George Harrison simply seems to have been baffled by it. McCartney once claimed that he discussed songwriting with Harrison and "he was saying that he didn't write songs the way I did . . . he said: 'I don't know how you write this ob-la-di, ob-la-da, Molly and Desmond, do you really know these people?' I said, 'No, I just make them up, like a novelist makes characters up.'"

It seems unlikely George Harrison really believed that Desmond and Molly were real people. Setting aside the disdain Harrison might have had for this fictionalized process, however, it's interesting to note that McCartney saw himself as writing like a novelist. Always the most "distant" of the Beatles, happy (unlike Lennon and Harrison) to write songs not born of personal experience, McCartney was never keen to expose his feelings and personal life in song (although he opened up a lot more after his marriage to Linda Eastman, which inspired him to write some of his most loving and heartfelt songs). Writing his character songs, he was able to be more comfortable and also to broaden his range as a lyricist—something Harrison never worried about, to his loss.

McCartney's songs about other people, imaginary or not, are far from patronizing (like Harrison's) and are rarely angry (like Lennon's). Distant he may have been, but McCartney—less egotistical and more sociable than some other Beatles—liked people and was interested in them. His best "character" song, "Eleanor Rigby," takes an observer's stance but, unlike Harrison's efforts in that direction (most notably "Piggies"), isn't patronizing.

Lyrically, "Ob-La-Di, Ob-La-Da" is well known for the happy accident near the end, where McCartney mixes up the song's protagonists Desmond and Molly and inadvertently turns Desmond into a ladyboy. It is also less well known that McCartney did not come up with the song's title (or, therefore, its refrain) himself. One of McCartney's friends at the time of the White Album sessions was a Nigerian conga player called Jimmy Anomuogharan Scott Emuakpor, known around London simply as Jimmy Scott. Scott's catchphrase for all occasions was a Yoruba expression he would instantly translate—ob-la-di, ob-la-da, life goes on. McCartney, enamored of this phrase, put it into a song. Despite being hired to play on the track, Scott was understandably unhappy about this, and some years later McCartney did send Scott—then playing with the U.K. ska revival band Bad Manners—a check to settle the matter. Sadly, Scott is now dead, effectively killed by British immigration officers. Reentering the United Kingdom, he was strip-searched by customs officials. By then a man in his 60s, he was then left naked in his cell for two hours. He died from pneumonia the next day.

Recorded July 3, 4, and 5 at Abbey Road. Overdubbed July 8, 9, 11, and 15.

Paul McCartney: lead vocals, bass
John Lennon: backing vocals, piano
George Harrison: backing vocals, acoustic guitar
Ringo Starr: drums
Jimmy Scott: maracas

Wild Honey Pie

(Credit: Lennon/McCartney. Actual writer: Paul McCartney)

The White Album has been criticized for being overlong and self-indulgent. This judgment is, essentially, nonsense, and it fails to take into account the fact that the charm and force of the White Album lies in part in its enormous, almost rambling scope and eclecticism. The record would be less extraordinary and special if it didn't veer from rock songs to crooner ballads and from pop tunes to tape-loop pieces designed to illustrate the apocalypse. No other band but the Beatles could encompass such a variety of music, whether it's of the highest quality or just engagingly daft (hi, Ringo). The White Album's impact relies on its untrammeled nature. Had it been reduced to a single album, it would just be another rock classic.

There is, however, one track that makes a convincing case for the trimming of the White Album, and that is track five, side one. Described by its composer as "a little experimental piece," "Wild Honey Pie" is no such thing, unless the experiment is one involving horrible torture. This track— brief as it is—duplicates almost exactly the experience of spending nearly a whole minute in Hades. Everything about it is irritating, from the plinky guitars, the falsetto vocals, and the clumpy moron drums to the stupid yodel at the end.

Many fans have voted this the second worst piece on the White Album, the worst being, predictably, "Revolution 9." That said, every one of "Revolution 9"'s experimental, over-criticized, and original eight minutes is better than the hellish 52 seconds of "Wild Honey Pie." That this track's self-indulgence, "humor," and false spontaneity would act as a blue-print for McCartney's early solo work is no excuse. You don't write a song like "Maybe I'm Amazed" dicking around like this. It may be no coincidence that McCartney wrote another song with virtually the same title shortly after, as if to remind himself that he didn't just knock out awful instrumentals with cute titles.

"Wild Honey Pie" started its horrible stunted life as an instrumental at Rishikesh, where its idiotic sound and comedic sing-along qualities made it, for some mysterious reason, a favorite of Patti Harrison. This seems little enough encourage-ment to put it on the White Album. Given that Patti Harrison was the inspiration for two of the best songs of their era, Eric Clapton's "Layla" and George Harrison's "Something," it's a shame that she's been given the blame for this tune.

"Wild Honey Pie" is the shortest track the Beatles ever recorded. Thank God.

Recorded August 20 at Abbey Road.

Paul McCartney: lead vocals, bass, backing vocals, drums, guitars

No other Beatles were harmed in the making of this song.

The Continuing Story of Bungalow Bill

(Credit: Lennon/McCartney. Actual writer: John Lennon)

One of the more unusual strands in Beatle songwriting was the story, or "character" song. McCartney tended to specialize in these, and on this album came up with "Rocky Raccoon" and the mini-soap of "Ob-La-Di, Ob-La-Da." Lennon was more dismissive of this kind of song, referring to McCartney's efforts in this area as songs about boring people with boring lives (ah, the empathy with the common man). He had rarely tried writing this kind of song himself, and his increasing belief in "honesty" and that only the truly personal can be truly art meant that he was the least likely Beatle to start making up songs about imaginary people. Most of Lennon's character songs—"Sexy Sadie," "Polythene Pam," and "Bungalow Bill"—are actually about real people (although no one has ever explained where the equally alliterative "Mean Mister Mustard" came from).

"Bungalow Bill" is, unsurprisingly, another Rishikesh song (it was demoed in Kinfauns directly after "Child of Nature," which, under the circumstances, makes perfect sense). The real progenitor of the song is the amazingly named Richard A. Cooke III, whose mother, Nancy Cooke, had been a follower of the Maharishi for some time, her interest predating that of the Beatles. Cooke had apparently visited the Rishikesh community to see his mother and while there had decided, with a lack of irony that only someone called Richard A. Cooke III could accomplish, to go tiger hunting. Taking his mother with him, Cooke actually shot a tiger that leapt at them both. Back at Rishikesh, Nancy Cooke began to recount the story, as one would. The Maharishi and his followers were clearly disturbed by it. Lennon intervened and asked Cooke if killing a tiger was not in some way "slightly life destructive." Cooke is supposed to have replied that it was either them or the tiger.

Lennon's questioning of Cooke's actions, Cooke's rationale, and the fact that he was accompanied by his mother on the hunt all ended up in the lyric, which drips sarcasm and irony. Unfortunately, "The Continuing Story of Bungalow Bill," for all its honesty and accuracy, is one of the dullest songs on the album. The production is murky and live, reflecting the way it was recorded, the melody draggy and a touch too ironic, and the chorus is an uninspired sing-along.

The song has its moments, as does every Lennon song. It contains one of his neatest comedy rhymes—"tiger hunting" with "elephant and"—and the title is pretty clever too, being a mixture of the names of the old fictional character Jungle Jim and, of course, Buffalo Bill. It displays an instinctive grasp of the portmanteau word, the invention of Lewis Carroll, Lennon's hero and influence. It was an early high point of producer Chris Thomas's career, as he got to play Mellotron as the rest of the Beatles performed the song. It also marks the appearance of the only female lead vocal on a Beatles record: when Yoko Ono sings Bill's mother's rejoinder (Ringo's wife, Maureen, is on backing vocals). None of these, however, lifts the song out of the hefty doldrums it squats in. It's a one-listen joke whose chorus really begins to annoy after a few minutes. Lennon was to perfect the subtle but direct character assassination song in his solo work, and had written better songs in this vein before. "Bungalow Bill" is a rare low point for him on this album.

Recorded October 8 at Abbey Road.

John Lennon: lead vocals, acoustic guitar, organ
Paul McCartney: backing vocals, bass
George Harrison: acoustic guitar, backing vocals
Ringo Starr: drums, tambourine, backing vocals
Yoko Ono: lead vocal, backing vocals
Maureen Starkey: backing vocals
Chris Thomas: Mellotron

While My Guitar Gently Weeps

(Harrison)

Ten songs into the Kinfauns demos, George Harrison finally gets to show off his own tunes in his own house. "While My Guitar Gently Weeps"—which takes its lyric, in the best I Ching-faced Beatles tradition, from a page in a book chosen at random—is one of the loveliest demos from the Kinfauns sessions. The song is fully realized as an acoustic number, and an acoustic version was even recorded for the White Album.

"While My Guitar Gently Weeps" has been criticized in recent years. It is a big bloaty thing in its final version, with a slightly patronizing lyric, and it doesn't really go anywhere. It's still a magnificent piece of work, however, and whatever its faults as an actual song, as a recording and a chunk of rock music, it works incredibly well. Harrison had never sounded so confident on record before, nor had he attempted such a powerful and emotive song. In creating "While My Guitar Gently Weeps," he also inadvertently invented '70s rock, which is arguably a bad thing but ensured the sale of small cigarette lighters for the next decade.

In its acoustic form, "While My Guitar Gently Weeps" is a delicate song, with a careful guitar part from Harrison and a quiet but oddly assertive vocal that is apparently at the upper limits of the guitarist's singing range but seems to suit his slightly adenoidal voice extremely well. The song's successive verses, marred slightly by the rather pedantic rhyme scheme—diverted/perverted/inverted/alerted being the most annoying quartet—at least try and make a point about the nature of existence, something Harrison was always keen to do. An extra verse, which had Harrison sitting on a stage watching the play that humanity was performing, was dropped. This was a good idea, as it added little to the song and would, in the final version, have made it supremely cumbersome (as well as over-emphasizing Harrison's view of himself as the dispassionate observer of all mankind's folly).

The final recorded version takes the controlled detachment of Harrison's acoustic song and turns it into a mighty wave of emotion. Harrison now stands on a mountain of sound and seems to look despairingly upon the world like an Old Testament prophet (only slightly more judgmental). And, as befits an epic, the playing, arrangements, and production are among the band's most striking. McCartney kicks the song off with a fantastic intro—a Morse-code piano that slips into the main riff—and his bass playing is superb and unusual, not the typical twisty McCartneyisms, but great fat portentous notes. Ringo's urgent percussion (castanets ahoy) makes the song virtually gallop, while Lennon's guitar playing rises to the occasion. The Beatles are all excellent on "While My Guitar Gently Weeps." They may, as Lennon claimed, be playing as each other's backing band, but they are a superb backing band.

Most notably, the song features a full wig-out rock guitar solo by the official emperor of the rock guitar solo, Eric Clapton. Clapton, an old friend of Harrison's, was brought in to play the solo that Harrison felt he couldn't achieve himself (he had tried, without success, to add a backward solo that sounded like weeping). It also lends the song some gravitas in the eyes of the other Beatles—if a proper guitarist like Eric Clapton liked it, it must be a proper song. The Beatles behaved, and Clapton—almost awed himself at playing on a Beatles album—did his work.

Eric Clapton remains unique in Beatle folklore as the only non-Beatle ever to play guitar on a Beatles record. There had been featured instrumentalists before: the Rolling Stones' Brian Jones had played saxophone on "You Know My Name (Look Up the Number)," classical musician Alan Civil had played French horn on "For No One," and there had been various sitar and tabla players on "Within You Without You" and other George Harrison compositions. On *Let It Be*, Harrison would bring in Billy Preston, but up until this point Eric Clapton was probably the only musician ever to play with the Beatles in such a featured and highlighted manner.

Clapton was brought in by Harrison partly to deflate the tension between the four members of the Beatles. Whenever there were other people around, particularly musicians whom they admired, the Beatles were notably better behaved. This suited everyone, but would have particularly made life much better for Harrison, whose struggle to have his songs accepted by Lennon and McCartney was constant. The presence on "While My Guitar Gently Weeps" of Eric

Clapton, a bona fide blues "god," lent weight to the song. In practical terms, it also meant that the rest of the band would at least pretend that they were playing on a "proper" song.

Clapton's presence here is slightly ironic, and one can only presume that friendship outweighed other considerations, as he was no friend to "pop" music. The former guitarist for John Mayall's Blues Breakers, a band of young white men devoted to playing fairly gripey versions of sexy songs by black Americans, Clapton stepped up to the Yardbirds, who at the time were a Rolling Stones-style band of bluesy rockers. When the Yardbirds' manager Giorgio Gomelsky decided to make his band more successful by hiring people outside the band to write songs for them (such as Graham Gouldman's superb "For Your Love"), Clapton objected to this blatant commercialization and left the group. The Yardbirds recruited Jeff Beck and Jimmy Page and went on to do new and interesting things with rock music. Eric Clapton, meanwhile, delved into the blues, only emerging to appear on this song, a tuneful affair from the greatest pop group in the world.

Clapton did well on his friend's song, despite having had initial doubts about being invited into a Beatles session. ("It's my song," Harrison told him, a little petulantly.) His blues sound, a little personalized and distinctive for a Beatles record, was treated with ADT (automatic double tracking, an effect that can be used to make instruments and vocal sounds "wobble"), which characterizes much of the band's later output. It also gives the song the extra portentousness and drama that Harrison presumably thought it needed (although some of its writer's own dry guitar playing might have deflated the song's world-weary pomposity a bit).

Eric Clapton was to continue to play a major role in George Harrison's life. In November, after the completion of the White Album, Harrison and Clapton wrote "Badge," which is full of Beatle-like arpeggios, for Clapton's band Cream. In 1969, sitting in Clapton's garden, Harrison came up with "Here Comes the Sun," for which millions are grateful. Then Harrison's wife, Patti Boyd, left him for Clapton. The theme of their unrequited love had already inspired Clapton's only great song, "Layla" (while Boyd and Clapton's realized relationship was responsible for the appalling "Wonderful Tonight"). Despite Harrison's feelings about the situation (which inspired a truly awful reworking of "Bye Bye Love," with references to "Clappers" going off with his woman), the two made up and remained friends until the end of Harrison's life. Clapton played on Harrison's last recorded live performances in Japan.

Trivia note. Harrison—despite being the Beatle who had the hardest time of all and might be expected to be the least nostalgic—had a musical habit of revisiting his time with the band. There was the splendid tribute to Lennon, "All Those Years Ago" (which also featured McCartney and Starr, and which contains a perfect pastiche of Lennon's bendy Flux Fiddlers string section as they appeared on his 1971 *Imagine* album). More recently, Harrison not only wrote the general 1960s/Beatles tribute "When We Were Fab," but also a song called "Here Comes the Moon." His nod to "While My Guitar Gently Weeps" was a track from the *Extra Texture* album called "This Guitar (Can't Keep from Crying)."

Recorded acoustically at Abbey Road July 25. Remade August 16. Overdubbed September 3. Remade again

September 5. Overdubbed again September 6.

George Harrison: lead vocals, acoustic guitar, organ
Paul McCartney: backing vocals, bass, piano, organ
John Lennon: lead guitar
Ringo Starr: drums, tambourine
Eric Clapton: lead guitar

Happiness Is a Warm Gun

(*Credit: Lennon/McCartney. Actual writer: John Lennon*)

The Beatles, as has been noted plenty of times in this book, had become each other's backing group on this album, rotating singers for each song like a studio-based showband. This situation helped to exacerbate tensions in the band, but it derived from each singer's desire to get his songs just so. In addition, because they were working in a studio, there was no need for, say, Harrison to play lead on a McCartney song, because McCartney could (and often did) play both bass and lead guitar on a song. That said, on "Happiness Is a Warm Gun," the Beatles buried their differences in one of their best musical, Beatles-as-band collaborations.

The song was famously put together from over 90 takes. It is a fiendishly tricky tune, changing tempo enough times in its few short minutes to satisfy the most crazed jazz composer, and is stylistically hugely varied. Lennon once claimed the song was "a history of rock 'n' roll." Presumably, he meant that it contained sections that were acid rock, doo-wop, and so forth. It's certainly a guide to different rock styles, and it basically creams every progressive rock song ever written with its sharp variability and sheer versatility.

The Beatles rose to the occasion magnificently, and were at their musical best throughout. Harrison and Lennon play knife-like guitar parts, which are distorted but controlled. McCartney offers enigmatic bass. Starr, given the almost-nightmarish task of steering the whole thing through its various time changes, is at his spartan best. (Always mocked for his simplicity as a drummer, Starr should in fact be knighted for it, and then made an Earl for refusing ever to play a drum solo. With his attitude, he could have saved drumming in the 1970s.)

For all its ensemble brilliance, "Happiness Is a Warm Gun" remains, however, an entirely Lennon song. No one else could have come up with its blend of strange but sharp imagery, creepy atmospherics, in-your-face stridency, muted menace, and jagged sexuality.

Lennon was effectively given the title for the song by George Martin. Martin showed him a gun magazine, on the cover of which were the words "Happiness Is a Warm Gun." No one, not even Martin, has ever explained what George Martin was doing with a gun magazine or why he showed it to Lennon. It seems as unlikely as the great man passing Lennon a copy of *Big Jugs* magazine. Posterity must assume that Martin saw the mag and realized that its cover caption was exactly the sort of thing to astonish and inspire John Lennon. If this was the case, it certainly worked. Like all cynics, Lennon was a man easily shocked. He thought the phrase was "a fantastic, insane thing to say," as "a warm gun means you've just shot something."

More than 30 years later, it's hard to say if the original magazine cover was as irony-free as history has it. What we do know is that the slogan owed its origins to, of all things, the Peanuts cartoons. In 1962, Charles M. Schulz published a collection of cartoons and homilies called *Happiness Is a Warm Puppy*, which in no way advocated shooting anyone, not even Charlie Brown. The gun magazine apparently picked up on this charming phrase some six years later (gun nuts obviously not being that quick on the draw), thus giving Lennon the most striking song title of his Beatle career.

The song is, to say the least, not directly about guns. It's a semi-narrative that begins as a collection of striking and disconcerting images—a lizard on a window pane, a man with mirrors on his boots, a soap impression of his wife. Lennon and Derek Taylor conjured up these images on an afternoon of free-associating (although the mirror man was real, being a Los Angeles pervert who liked to look up girls' dresses with his boot-based reflectors). The internal semi-rhyme of "ate" and "donated" is a notable part of the genuine surrealism of the last line of the verse, and the whole section is menacing, unreal, and even Dali-esque, one of the many examples of Lennon using apparently meaningless language to create a strong emotional effect.

The second part of "Happiness Is a Warm Gun" is the superb heavy section, whose references to "a fix" and "Mother Superior" are free associations related to drug language and to Lennon's nickname for Yoko Ono, "Mother." While admitting to the mother/Ono link, Lennon always denied the song was about drugs, even though he'd also just written "Everybody's Got Something to Hide Except Me and My Monkey" whose last word is also heroin slang. (Paul McCartney also asserts that this was written during the period that Lennon was using heroin.) He also claimed, with obvious sincerity, that the rest of the song was just "images" of Yoko

Ono. The third part of the song is a doo-wop pastiche, with more alarming lyrics than most hits of that era. References to holding Ono in his arms and feeling his hand on her trigger stem from the fact that, as Lennon said, "that was the beginning of my relationship with Yoko and I was very sexually oriented then. When we weren't in the studio, we were in bed."

At this stage in his career, Lennon had still not abandoned his belief in the usefulness of poetic imagery and the notion that truth can be found in random, apparently nonsensical lyrics. Acid and common sense also told him that it was, in fact, no crime to write songs that create an atmosphere rather than tell a conventional story or put across a point of view. He was sadly to abandon this approach throughout the 1970s, which meant that songs called "Power to the People," "Woman," and "Cold Turkey" were actually about giving power to the people, a woman, and cold turkey—the drug withdrawal kind, that is, not the dead bird kind. (Paradoxically, under Lennon's influence—notably his insistence that lines like "the movement you need is on your shoulder" improved his songs, which they did—Paul McCartney went the other way in the 1970s, filling his songs with an almost nursery rhyme-like jumble of meaningless half-stories, silly characters, and childish chatter. Thus a fine lyrical talent was lost for several years, and a McCartney lyric became pleasurable to listen to again only when he summoned Elvis Costello to his side on the 1989 album *Flowers in the Dirt*.)

"Happiness Is a Warm Gun" has been covered by a few artists, most recently and notably Tori Amos, who picked up on its extraordinary blend of violence and sexuality. In addition, ironists have not been slow to make connection between the song's title and origin and the fact that John Lennon was murdered with a handgun. In 2000, shortly after the twentieth anniversary of Lennon's murder, Yoko Ono led a gun control campaign prior to the U.S. presidential election. She told the press, "John, who was the king of the world and had everything any man could ever want, came back to me in a brown paper bag in the end."

Recorded September 23 and 24 at Abbey Road. Overdubbed September 25.

John Lennon: lead vocals, lead guitar, backing vocals
Paul McCartney: backing vocals, bass
George Harrison: lead guitar, backing vocals
Ringo Starr: drums

SIDE TWO

Martha My Dear

(Credit: Lennon/McCartney. Actual writer: Paul McCartney)

Ushering in the slightly more thoughtful perkiness that would characterize his solo work, McCartney wrote a song that many find annoying for its oddly inconclusive feel and musical circularity. Some fans believe "Martha My Dear" to be about the end of his affair with Jane Asher, or about a liaison with some unnamed woman. Most are aware that it's really a song about his Old English sheepdog. "Martha My Dear" is full of charm, tunefulness, and a splendid, deeply McCartneyesque piano riff. Like its writer, the piano line seems to have a permanently raised eyebrow, whether in quizzical acknowledgment of life's ups and downs or simply in wry astonishment at the composer's musical abilities. In fact, it began life as a piano exercise, and arguably never quite evolved from that.

With its middle eight, in which McCartney exhorts his sheepdog to take a good look around her, "Martha My Dear" seems to echo Lennon's "Dear Prudence." The "around 'round" section of Lennon's song is exultantly dizzy and kind of cosmic, however, while its equivalent in "Martha My Dear" is slightly smug in both intent and execution. The addition of brass adds little more than some moderately stiff rhythm to the song, and it relies largely on McCartney's technical excellence, lovely voice, and that teasing piano to keep listeners interested.

McCartney—keen in interviews, possibly for dry, comedic reasons, to emphasize that his relationship with Martha the sheepdog was "purely platonic"—has never made great claims for this song, but its inspiration (the sheepdog) did play an important part in his life. In interviews about his passions—animal rights and vegetarianism—he talks about the fact that as a child he never had a pet, and that Martha was the first animal he had ever owned. The dog kindled McCartney's love of animals, an interest that was to flourish when he met, and later married, Linda Eastman. So there is genuine affection and love in what many people tend to dismiss as a silly song.

Trivia fans will be delighted to learn that Paul later owned "two cats called Pyramis and Thisbe, which showed my literate bent" and after that, a trio of cats called Jesus, Mary, and Joseph. He must have had fun calling them in at night.

Recorded October 4 and 5 at Abbey Road.

Paul McCartney: vocals, bass, drums, lead guitar
Brass section

I'm So Tired

(Credit: Lennon/McCartney. Actual writer: John Lennon)

One of the greatest of John Lennon's songs and certainly the funniest, "I'm So Tired" is a perfect exercise in mood, pace, and melody. It's also the only song ever written that manages not only to musically describe insomnia, but to also make it sound entertaining.

"I'm So Tired" was the fourth song to be demoed at Kinfauns, in a superb, energetic, and dry version that had its lyric, arrangement, and even vocal performance already in place. Lennon's falsetto voice sounds as weary as possible, and the eruption from the "You'd say . . ." section into the sleepless man's desperate plea—"I'd give you everything I've got for a little peace of mind!" is perfect, the exact aural equivalent of losing it in a big way with the duvet. Lennon sounds enthusiastic throughout, even yelping during the song's climaxes. On this demo version, he added a spoken passage (the first line of which was reworked for the last verse of "Happiness Is a Warm Gun")—"When I hold you in your arms/When you show each one of your charms/I wonder should I get up and go to the funny farm?" He ended the song with an aside presumably aimed at Apple press nabob Derek Taylor—"I'll give you everything I've got, Derek."

At Abbey Road, the rest of the Beatles were equally enthused by the song and produced an excellent arrangement. Harrison in particular added some superbly jagged lead guitar. Starr drummed impeccably, a mixture of sluggishness and thunder wherever appropriate. McCartney was also slinky and, as ever, intelligent in his playing. Lennon simply gave the performance of his career, moving from inertia to a droll final mumble. Millions have tried to decipher that final mumble. Some rather optimistic-eared fans claim that Lennon is saying "monsieur, monsieur, let's have another, please, please" which fits the mood of the song like a glove fits a foot. More notably—and much, much more stupidly—this is the section that, if played backward, apparently sounds like "Paul is dead, miss him, miss him." This is nonsense. To be blunt, Lennon doesn't say that. Play the track forward, and it's clear that Lennon is just mumbling. Play it backward, and it's clear that he's mumbling backward.

Aside from mumbles, "I'm So Tired" is full of real, intentional great lyrics. The best of these is generally agreed to be the "curse Sir Walter Raleigh" verse, which not only contains a vicious attack on the man who brought tobacco to Europe, but also introduced the word "get" (the Liverpool version of the popular British insult "git") to the world language pool. (It's also responsible for the rather dramatic mondegreen, or lyrical mishearing, "and curse the walls around me/I'm such a stupid get.")

Written in India, not surprisingly, when Lennon couldn't sleep, "I'm So Tired" is an installment in one of John Lennon's personal sub-genres, the sleep song. Like many artistic people who rise late, work late, and value their sleep perhaps a little too much, Lennon was mad for his bed. He conducted his relationship with Ono in bed. ("The Ballad of John and Yoko" even contains a line about "the wife" talking to Lennon "in bed.") His great political gesture was the bed-in, which was done partly for its humor value, partly because, on some level, bed must have appeared to Lennon a much more sensible place to be than Vietnam, and partly because he just liked being in bed. His first solo single, "Give Peace a Chance," is one of the few classic songs actually recorded in bed. (If you want to push this concept, and I do, even on 1965's "Norwegian Wood," the listener sometimes wonders if Lennon didn't burn down the woman's house because he'd had to sleep in the bath.)

The first great Lennon sleep song was, naturally, "I'm Only Sleeping," the flip side of "I'm So Tired." There, Lennon seems to happily drift off in a careless daze, not interested in the rest of the world and not caring that he's not interested. The song positively sails along, and is one of Lennon's loveliest. (It was also, weirdly, a minor hit for the ex-Madness vocalist Suggs.) "I'm So Tired" starts in a way that is reminiscent of "I'm Only Sleeping," but drags along where the other floats. Then "I'm So Tired" becomes loud and irritated, a harsh rock song born out of something more feather-light.

Lennon's other connection to sleep was his emotional investment in dream worlds. This album's "Cry Baby Cry" has that dream-like quality, as does the wafting "Julia." Conversely, the sound of "Revolution 9" is that of a nightmare. And in his solo work, the Rishikesh soppiness of "Child of Nature" was reworked into "Jealous Guy" with its opening line, "I was dreaming of the past," while "Number Nine Dream" feels exactly like a waking dream.

Lennon—the man who firmly told the world that the Beatles, and the 1960s, were ended with the phrase "the dream is over"—epitomizes the artist in the Beatles, the creative person who strikes when the muse is hot, and cannot work when inspiration is absent. True or not—Lennon could work like hell when the moment was upon him—the perception has gained hold that Lennon was the artistic one, and that McCartney was the "craftsman," the Beatle who, for a consideration, could knock you out a nice little song on commission. And while there is some truth in this—for Paul McCartney took justifiable pride in the fact that he was able to turn out a theme song for Cilla Black here and a hit single for Badfinger there—it denigrates McCartney's own genius. A man visited by melodies as perfect as "Yesterday" and "Blackbird" and by an imagination as powerful as that displayed on "Back in the U.S.S.R." and "Penny Lane" is not to be dismissed as some kind of hack.

While McCartney's views are not known on the subject of the artist/craftsman divide—the chasm between the creative muse-inspired type and the plodding hard worker—he is deeply fed up with the notion that Lennon was the experimental, inspired one and he wasn't. Perhaps this is best summed up by McCartney's somewhat tart comment regarding "I'm So Tired": "I think we were all pretty tired, but he chose to write about it."

Recorded October 8 at Abbey Road.

John Lennon: lead vocals, lead and acoustic guitars, organ, backing vocals
Paul McCartney: backing vocals, bass
George Harrison: lead and rhythm guitars
Ringo Starr: drums

Blackbird

(Credit: Lennon/McCartney. Actual writer: Paul McCartney)

One of Paul McCartney's best songs, "Blackbird" is also one of his own favorites. He has rerecorded the song on two live albums, the 1976 *Wings Over America* collection and the 1991 *Unplugged* set. In 2001, McCartney named his collected poetry and lyrics book *Blackbird Singing*, after the song. (There's also the possibility that *Band on the Run*'s cute "Bluebird" is a deliberate titular reference to "Blackbird.") A Rishikesh number, its finger-picking style makes it one of the acoustic Beatles songs written under the musical influence of fellow attendee Donovan Leitch. Donovan's previous contribution to the Beatles' work had been the lines "sky of blue, sea of green" in "Yellow Submarine." Now he was exerting a different influence. In Rishikesh, Donovan's acoustic guitar skills and knowledge of the British folk tradition—which the Beatles had nothing to do with what-soever—came to the fore.

With no instruments in India but their acoustic guitars, the Beatles were forced to write songs in that idiom, and were interested to learn Donovan's playing techniques. In fact, Donovan probably also saved them from a certain degree of musical boredom, if a 1968 Italian TV documentary is anything to go by. The Beatles and friends are filmed enjoying a campfire sing-along. While Donovan is able to play his own "Catch the Wind" and Dylan's "Blowin' in the Wind," the Beatles—the greatest songwriters in the world—are reduced to entertaining the small crowd with the likes of "Jingle Bells" and "When the Saints Go Marching In." Armed with the new (to them) techniques that Donovan had taught them, the

Beatles were able to increase their musical range substantially. Songs such as Lennon's "Julia" and "Dear Prudence," Harrison's "While My Guitar Gently Weeps," and McCartney's "Mother Nature's Son" came directly from this time. The best song of that period, however, was only indirectly—if strongly—inspired by Rishikesh.

Actually composed on McCartney's farm in Scotland, "Blackbird" was performed, as often happened on the White Album, solely by McCartney, its only accompaniment a "ticking" sound (which may be a metronome, or just McCartney's tapping foot) and, more notably, a sound archive recording of a blackbird chirping. (McCartney later said that the blackbird did a "pretty good job.") "Blackbird" was inspired by an unknown piece of Bach, generally assumed to be part of the minuet that also inspired the Toys' early 1960s girl group single "A Lover's Concerto." J. S. Bach was all the rage in 1968, having provided the musical engine for Procol Harum's enormous hit single, "A Whiter Shade of Pale." His baroque stylings had been the wellspring for the plethora of cornets and tinny trumpets on virtually every single Beatles tune, from "Penny Lane" to "It's All Too Much." According to McCartney, both he and Harrison had been intrigued by Bach from an early age, even learning Bach pieces and later, as the Beatles became famous, deciding that Bach was their kind of composer. "We felt we had a lot in common with him," McCartney said later. "For some reason, we thought his music was very similar to ours." The Beatles were also impressed with the idea of Bach "being the church organist and wopping this stuff out weekly," something that would appeal to McCartney's sense of workmanship.

The song's gorgeous melody, set to an extraordinary guitar tuning, is atmospheric enough, but the lyric takes it in a whole new direction. The sources for the song's inspiration are, as things tend to be, diverse and conflicting. It's generally assumed to initially have been inspired by the sound of an actual blackbird singing outside McCartney's window and waking him up. This gels with the song's sense of awakening and the music's extraordinary sense of positive tension and anticipation. It's also been claimed that the song is a tribute to the American Civil Rights movement. Certainly the word "blackbird" crops up a great deal in the civil rights literature of the period, and a musical called *Fly Blackbird Fly* was performed in front of Martin Luther King, Jr. This may have had some influence on the song's naming. While some commentators have expressed doubt about this claim, it has had a lot of retrospective effect. In recent years, Paul McCartney himself has frequently asserted that when he wrote the song, he "had in mind a black woman, rather than a bird." He says now that he wrote "Blackbird" as a song to an imaginary black woman in the United States, to encourage and bring hope, and that, being McCartney, he veiled the song's specific lyrical thrust to give it a universality to enable it to apply to people in general.

Concerning the memories of individual Beatles, it can sometimes be difficult to say whether they are recalling something they felt or did at the time, or whether they are mixing up other people's more attractive theories about what happened with what actually did occur. Nevertheless, McCartney seems very definite on this point. Certainly, the song has had a powerful effect on thousands of people, who—McCartney points out—have taken consolation and been given hope by the song. And retrospective inspiration, after all, is still inspiration.

The song was also tied into McCartney's newfound mood of optimism. The night Linda Eastman moved into McCartney's London home, he sat on the window sill of his top floor music room and played the song to the fans who camped outside his front gate—a beautiful and thrilling moment that most of us would love to have been present at.

Recorded June 11 at Abbey Road.

Paul McCartney: lead vocals, acoustic guitar

Piggies

(Harrison)

George Harrison's position in the Beatles was always reflected by the number of his compositions on each Beatles album. On early albums he was lucky to get a single song—sometimes he would end up singing a cover, such as "Roll Over Beethoven," or even a Lennon/McCartney song, such as "I'm Happy Just to Dance with You" (a lyric his lugubrious scouse delivery rather gave the lie to). As a composer, he was a variable and often disinterested-seeming talent. From the earliest Harrison song to appear on a record, the sullen but catchy "Don't Bother Me," to *Sgt. Pepper's* cosmically epic "Within You Without You," Harrison seemed limited by both his smaller vocal range and, more significantly, by the other two writers in the band.

John Lennon and Paul McCartney, for all their wit, intelligence, and personal charm, were not always the easiest people to be with. (Lennon, perhaps exaggerating, once described the Beatles as "the biggest bastards in the world.") Even their inner circle was not immune to criticism and sharp Liverpool sarcasm. In the area of songwriting, they could be extremely ungenerous. In the *Let It Be* movie, there is a scene in which Harrison is rehearsing "I Me Mine," and as he plays it, Lennon loudly sings the chorus of "Taste of Honey," a song with a slight melodic similarity to Harrison's.

Getting a song on a Beatles album was an uphill struggle if you weren't Lennon or McCartney, and George Harrison—despite being, nominally, an equal partner in the band—wrote barely 10 percent of the 200-plus songs recorded by the Beatles (and of the twenty or so songs the Beatles gave away to other artists, only one—"Sour Milk Sea," recorded by Jackie Lomax—was written by Harrison). Younger than the other Beatles—and always regarded by them as "a kid"—Harrison must be one of the few lead guitarists ever to have bonded with the band's drummer as a fellow secondary band member. (This goes some way to explaining the unusual pairing of Harrison and Starr as songwriters both at this time and in the early 1970s.) He was also not only competing with the two best songwriters in the world, but also with two men prepared to fight their corner. Lennon and McCartney, skills honed to a knife's edge from competition with each other, were quite prepared to swat off Harrison's lesser efforts in the most casual manner.

After the Beatles split up, Harrison's creative dam burst, and he produced the enormous *All Things Must Pass* album, three discs of religious fervor, Bob Dylan collaborations, live tracks, Phil Spector productions, and heartfelt (if often variable) music. While his songwriting confidence had been growing—Abbey Road features both "Something" and "Here Comes the Sun," perhaps his two best Beatles (and most Beatlesque) songs—there had been nothing to indicate that Harrison was about to fill acres of vinyl with confident, idiosyncratic music. The truth, as interviews from the era indicate, was that Harrison had more or less given up submitting—the word is totally appropriate—his songs to the rest of the band.

The White Album is an exception. Fresh from India, where, in a sense, he had briefly been the band's spiritual leader, Harrison had, like the rest of the band, several songs stockpiled. His songwriting abilities were just coming to fruition. There would be no gloomy plods like the funereal "Blue Jay Way" and, oddly, no more sideways slips into Indian-style pop like the great "Love You To." Harrison's interest in India and his exploration of Indian music did give him a new, strengthened place in the band for a while. Inevitably, however, this would have been a musical cul-de-sac, and Harrison's solo records—conventional pop rock—show that he, too, realized this. It was one thing to promote his mentor Ravi Shankar's music; it was another to play it.

At the end of the Kinfauns demo tapes, George got his turn to play. He's heard offering the band the beautiful, acoustic version of "While My Guitar Gently Weeps" and four other songs: "Circles," "Sour Milk Sea," "Not Guilty," and "Piggies." It is a measure of Harrison's position in the band that, while virtually all of Lennon and McCartney's songs from this session appear on the White Album, Harrison's strike rate was only two out of five. (McCartney's "Junk" and Lennon's "Child of Nature" would appear pretty quickly on their solo albums, while Harrison's "Not Guilty" and "Circles" would vanish for a decade.) This means that old toot such as "Rocky Raccoon" and "Bungalow Bill" were ultimately preferred over Harrison's edgy "Not Guilty" and excellent "Sour Milk Sea." ("Circles" is less successful, being an aptly named spiral through some of Harrison's favorite minor chords. Though slightly spooky and atmospheric, its job was done much better by Harrison's "Long, Long, Long," which did make the album.) "Circles" and "Not Guilty" eventually appeared in modified versions on Harrison solo records many years later, and Jackie Lomax recorded "Sour Milk Sea." "While My Guitar Gently Weeps" went from being a delicate acoustic song to a rock epic. However, the last song of Harrison's that was demoed at Kinfauns, "Piggies," journeyed from demo to White Album track in relatively unchanged form.

"Piggies" is an unusual song for Harrison. Despite being a moral lesson for the world, this time the moral is expressed in the form of metaphor; the human race are compared to pigs. This is always a popular theme in literature and art. It was done well by George Orwell in *Animal Farm* and badly by Pink Floyd on its *Animals* album. Harrison's piggies are seemingly divided into two types: the little piggies, who are presumably most of us, in the dirt and with ever-worsening lives, and the big piggies, who wear shirts and take their wives to dinner, and who go around "stirring up the dirt."

As a coherent critique of society, it's pretty feeble. Musically, however, "Piggies" is a powerful song, full of angry climaxes (the "damn good whacking" moment is particularly melodramatic, as Harrison suddenly looms over the horizon like a wrathful God) and snaky, sardonic verses. Vocally, it's a fine performance, full of irony and disdain, and, if it wasn't a song that completely dismisses the human race out of hand, "Piggies" would even be funny. It has a charming baroque feel, some delicate guitar work, and a nifty harpsichord break by the young Chris Thomas. There's a nice shift to rock in the "in the skies with all their backing" section (although what the hell does that line mean? Aerial financial backing?) and some cute menace in the song's last line, where the pigs are off to eat some bacon. (The original last line was changed, probably at Lennon's suggestion, from the rather feeble and virtually unsingable "to cut their pork chops." Before that it was even worse, being some nonsense about going to piggy banks to give piggy thanks "to thee, pig brother.")

"Piggies" is an unpleasant song. It does form part of a venerable British rock tradition of sneering at the middle classes, whose crimes generally seem to include, in the suburban English rock/pop tradition, having jobs, going to their jobs on trains, owning umbrellas, and so forth. However, it's nastier than that, encompassing the whole of humanity who, Harrison asserts, need to be punished because they are not interested in what's going on around them. It's an arrogant song, showing the dark side of Harrison's religiosity, where the unenlightened are just the ones too stupid to get their names on the guest list, and where the enlightened sit around cross-legged all day looking down on the rest of us in the dirt. Although the Beatles preached peace and love and meant it, large parts of the White Album indicate that they could be a bit selective about it.

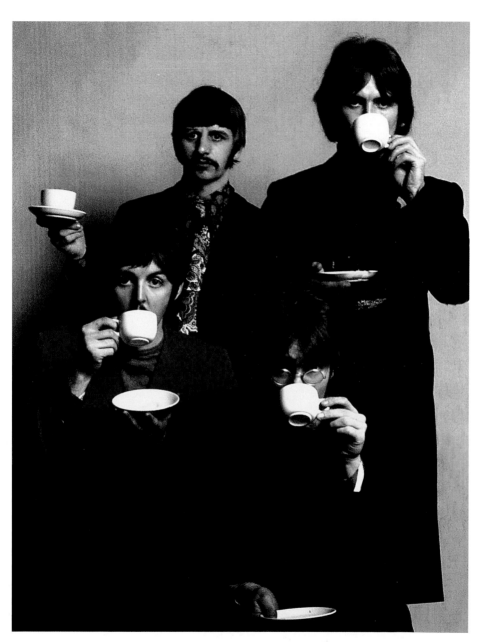

Between dropping acid and smoking dope, the Beatles find time for a rare tea break.

Left *Victoria Hall, Bradford, June 30, 1968: Four days after recording "Everybody's Got Something to Hide Except Me and My Monkey" with the Beatles, the ever-eclectic Paul McCartney conducts the Black Dyke Mills Band on "Thingumybob," released as an Apple single.*

Left *Ringo Starr wearing a hat in his first film,* Candy.

Right *1960s rivals*
John Lennon and
Mick Jagger compare
psychedelic jackets.

Left *George Harrison*
frightening himself on
a trumpet.

Left *Yoko Ono ("Ocean Child") and John Lennon, minutes away from giving peace a chance.*

Left *George Martin contemplates another laughter-filled day recording the White Album.*

Above *George Harrison's fascination with India gave him influence in the Beatles for the first time.*

Above *The Beatles and the Maharishi, obviously ecstatic about meeting each other.*

*Left Eric Clapton,
about to play on*
While My Guitar
Gently Weeps,
*have an affair with
George's wife, become
a junkie, etc.*

Left *Donovan
Leitch, acoustic
folkie powerhouse
and White Album
guitar guru.*

The Beatles, practicing different facial expressions for their solo careers.

No matter how jaundiced and negative his view of human life was in this song, Harrison cannot be blamed for its effect on the evil lunatic Charles Manson. A later chapter deals with this in more detail.

Recorded September 19 at Abbey Road. Overdubbed September 20 and October 10.

George Harrison: lead vocals, acoustic guitar
Paul McCartney: bass
John Lennon: tape loops
Ringo Starr: tambourine
Chris Thomas: harpsichord
Strings

Rocky Raccoon

(Credit: Lennon/McCartney. Actual writer: Paul McCartney)

In a classic bit of White Album segueing, after a burst of pig grunting, acoustic chords introduce "Rocky Raccoon," another bowl of McCartney whimsy and not one of his greats. While not a bad song, and certainly the equal of Lennon's more focused (much more focused) "Bungalow Bill," "Rocky Raccoon" is a long, rambling journey toward what is supposed to be a punchline but in reality is just a smartypants pun.

Written in Rishikesh and probably very popular around the campfire at night, this song does not work well on record. Comedy songs—for that is what "Rocky Raccoon" most resembles, having no other content—rarely stand up to repeated listening, their effectiveness generally being in their lyrics, which, like most jokes, become less funny with repetition. The track's narrative sounds like the kind of thing that someone might have made up on the spot and worked on later. In fact, it's also a parody song, though of something that most of its modern listeners may not ever come across.

McCartney has described the song as "a Mack Sennett movie set to music," and while it does come across as a comedic western tune, its roots are not silent movie slapstick, but vaudeville. The lyric of "Rocky Raccoon" uses the rhyme schemes of traditional music hall recitations, but lacks their barmy energy. It's a half-remembered remake of an old-style vaudeville recitation, in this case Robert W. Service's old warhorse, "The Shooting of Dan McGrew," which also features characters called Dan and Lil (in Service's poem, she is "known as Lil," in the song she "called herself Lil"). But where Service's poem is a melodramatic, overwrought, and powerful piece about love and betrayal, "Rocky Raccoon" is a silly song about nothing. Even the music seems disinterested in its mission, as each line seems to fade away, almost in embarrassment, and the repetitive riff warns the listener that nothing is going to happen. George Martin's cheery honky-tonk piano coda sounds not so much as though it's concluding the song as it is leading it off into police custody.

As a humorous lyricist, McCartney is often excellent—in his hands, a song like, for example, "Lovely Rita," can be a delightfully daft sketch—but here he seems content to come up with the odd clever rhyme and the much-overrated final joke about Gideon and his bible. The song, an ironic parody of something that, by 1968, was a bit late for parodying, is an example of McCartney trying an experiment with form that should have been hidden away in a big jar afterward.

The song was originally called "Rocky Sassoon," either after the war poet Siegfried Sassoon, or—which is more likely—the hairdresser Vidal Sassoon. Its Kinfauns version contained slightly different lyrics. But nothing about any of these was better or worse than the final, fairly forgettable, White Album version.

Recorded August 15 at Abbey Road

Paul McCartney: lead vocals, acoustic guitar
John Lennon: backing vocals, bass, harmonium, harmonica
George Harrison: backing vocals
Ringo Starr: drums
George Martin: honky-tonk piano

Don't Pass Me By

(Starkey)

Although he had been friends with Lennon, McCartney, and Harrison for several years and had even sat in with the Beatles for several live shows, Ringo Starr was the last person to join the band. He replaced Pete Best virtually hours before the band went into the studio to make their first record, "Love Me Do." Significantly, Starr was not allowed by George Martin to play on the version of "Love Me Do" that came out as a single. Starr was also the only Beatle ever to be replaced, when he fell ill in 1965 and the band hired a substitute drummer called Jimmy Nicol (whose son ended up working with the Beatles on the TV version of *Anthology*. They keep their friends close to them, the Beatles, and their ex-drummers even closer.) And, in 1968, Starr was the first Beatle to walk out, after being told by McCartney how to play drums on "Back in the U.S.S.R." (On that occasion, he was replaced behind the kit by Paul McCartney.)

Being Ringo was not an easy job. Mocked affectionately for his looks—and for his rings, which perhaps he wore to deflect attention from remarks about his nose and bloodhound eyes—Starr was also mocked less affectionately for his unconventional drumming technique. Jokes about his skill as a drummer ignored the fact that Starr was, and is, a superb and individual player (Beatles songs on which he does not play lack a certain energy), and must have been hurtful. In a band where two members were popularly and critically acclaimed as geniuses on a daily basis, and where one was thought to be a bit of a guru on the quiet, being the funny one must have been a burden more than once.

As a member of a touring band, Starr was a happier man on the road. Like everyone else on stage, he was an essential part of the group (and was even, like all of the other Beatles, a visual focus, with his elevated kit and extraordinary "dancing" playing style). In the two years before the White Album, however, the Beatles had retired from live work, and Starr found himself in the tedious position of being the drummer for a studio band. While Lennon, McCartney, and even Harrison worked on new and imaginative—and time-consuming—ideas for *Revolver* and *Sgt. Pepper*, Starr spent hours and hours playing cards with the road crew, Mal Evans and Neil Aspinall.

All this goes some way to explaining why Starr's first recorded composition—not counting material on which he was cocredited, such as the country and western tune "What

Goes On" and the instrumental "Flying"—should be called "Don't Pass Me By." While the actual lyric is a simplistic (and slightly lurid) plea for romantic acceptance, its intent has been seen by some commentators as a request to not be ignored in the Beatles. Equally significant, the song's title, while not necessarily being attached to this particular tune, had been around since 1963, which pretty much indicates that Ringo had been feeling insecure for a long time.

On record, "Don't Pass Me By" is arguably the kind of song that would have been dropped if the White Album had been a single, but most listeners are glad that it wasn't. "Don't Pass Me By" is a slightly clumsy, basic song, with a lolloping rhythm that comes from its composer's distinctly drummer-like piano playing. It has a daft and charming lyric, and it achieves, as all Ringo's songs do, an effect of complete sincerity. Its country and western feel—which it shares with "What Goes On" and Starr's earlier cover of "Act Naturally"— indicates where Starr's heart really lay. In the midst of some of the most extraordinary and experimental music of all time, Starr was a traditionalist who was unafraid to follow his own path. His second solo album, *Beaucoups of Blues*, was actually recorded in Nashville and is a fine late-1960s country album.

Starr was to develop as a songwriter. His two notable Harrison collaborations, "Octopus's Garden" and the solo tune "Photograph," are as good as most Beatles songs, and his solo albums before 1974 are all worth investigating. Beatle lovers are advised in particular to check out the song "Early 1970," a gentle but sharply observed look at his three band members. His solo recording career slowed down faster than those of the other Beatles, and despite some excellent comeback albums, Starr is now best known as an ex-Beatle and, in Britain, as the man who did the voice-over for the children's animated series "Thomas the Tank Engine."

"Don't Pass Me By" was recorded between the sessions for "Revolution 1" and "Revolution 9," which must have been weird. It was released as a single in Scandinavia. During recording, it went under two other titles: "Ringo's Tune (Untitled)" and, more peculiarly, "This Is Some Friendly," which was later used by the British band the Charlatans for an album title.

Recorded June 5 at Abbey Road. Overdubbed June 6, July 12 and 22.

Ringo Starr: lead vocals, drums, piano
Paul McCartney: bass, piano
Jack Fallon: violin

Why Don't We Do It in the Road?

(Credit: Lennon/McCartney. Actual writer: Paul McCartney)

John Lennon was the rude Beatle, the one who made statements about being bigger than God and who was prone to making off-color remarks about disabled people. He posed naked for an album sleeve and married a foreigner. No wonder, then, that virtually everyone who hears "Why Don't We Do It in the Road?" for the first time assumes that it's a John Lennon song. It seems logical that he should write the Beatles' most blatant and outrageous song about sex.

By way of contrast, Paul McCartney was "the cute one" of the Beatles. With his enormous eyes, quizzical eyebrows, and cozy manner, he was the Beatle most likely to settle down with a nice lady and write musicals featuring songs like "Yesterday" and "When I'm 64." In fact, McCartney was also into avant-garde art before John Lennon. It was he who inserted the phrase "finger pie" into "Penny Lane," and he was the first Beatle to go public about his drug use. (He's still publicizing it, in fact, having ended 2001 by telling the British rock magazine Q that he once took cocaine for a year.) And, of course, he was the Beatle who wrote "Why Don't We Do It in the Road?"

Inspired by the sight of monkeys having sex in Rishikesh and thoughts of the basic nature of the sex act, "Why Don't We Do It in the Road?" is one of the most popular Beatles album tracks. Its lyric is probably the shortest one in their canon, consisting of the title and the phrase "no one will be watching us" repeated several times in different orders. Set to a driving beat—all hand claps, staccato drumming from McCartney (and Starr, whose part was added later as an over-dub), and a frugging piano—"Why Don't We Do It in the Road?" is a simple joke song that rewards the listener time and time again, from its intro clapping to McCartney's final, abrupt twisting of the title phrase. It is, in short, a Beatles classic, except for the fact that the Beatles aren't actually on it.

Recorded in a corridor when Lennon and Harrison were elsewhere working on final mixes, "Why Don't We Do It in the Road?" was a fun piece of work for McCartney and is indicative of the nature of his early solo work—simple, effective, and all the parts played by one man who was in no way a control freak. Harrison later claimed that the reason songs were recorded when other Beatles were known to be absent was simply because time was short and the album had to be finished. This doesn't adequately explain, however, why McCartney would suddenly take it upon himself make a solo recording of a new song for the one Beatles album that was unarguably not short of material. Tensions were high at this point, and it's generally assumed that McCartney deliberately excluded the other Beatles.

Whether or not this is true, John Lennon certainly believed it to be the case. On several occasions, he mentioned his displeasure at being excluded from the recording, always leaving open the implication that McCartney was being selfish, or an egomaniac, or just a bad person, by doing so. (McCartney, for his part, likes to point out that he was excluded—as were the other Beatles—from the recording of "Revolution 9." It's a fair point, regardless of the fact that McCartney is unlikely to have wanted to be there for the recording of "Revolution 9.") Most likely, Lennon was envious. "Why Don't We Do It in the Road?" is not only a great song, but it's one that Lennon, as most listeners have noted, could easily have written or recorded himself. Sour grapes or not, this song remains one of the sharpest, most succinct, and funniest rockers that any of the Beatles ever recorded. And the fact that McCartney recorded it on John Lennon's 28th birthday may be the real reason that Lennon was so peeved.

Recorded October 9 and 10 at Abbey Road.

Paul McCartney: lead vocals, guitar, piano, drums
Ringo Starr: drums

I Will

(Credit: Lennon/McCartney. Actual writer: Paul McCartney)

Millions have been entertained by the juxtaposition of this song's title and the one before it, and we may never know if it was deliberate or not. Equally uncertain is the rationale for the placing of the two songs side by side. There could not be a better illustration of the poles of Paul McCartney's songwriting abilities than these two songs. "Why Don't We Do It in the Road?" is a McCartney rocker, sexy, succinct, and funny. "I Will" is doe-eyed Paul, all croonsome voice, lovely harmonies, romantic lyrics, and a tune that all but whistles itself.

"I Will" is the White Album's token romantic ballad ("Blackbird" and "Mother Nature's Son" being something else entirely). It is also one of the last of this kind of song that Paul McCartney would write for the band. (George Harrison provided, in a kind of out-of-left-field way, the band's last great love song.) He was to return to this style of writing in his solo career ("Maybe I'm Amazed," "My Love"), but for now McCartney seems to have largely abandoned the form.

This was possibly because his relationship with Jane Asher—which had inspired much of his early romantic work—was ending, and he might have become fed up with writing soppy tunes, but it seems clear from the facile nature of "I Will" that the form was no longer exciting him. And this is a shame. As a balladeer, McCartney had always been unbeatable. (Lennon did not really master this technique until his final album with Yoko Ono, the mature, and often McCartneyesque *Double Fantasy*.) He was, after all, the man who had written "Yesterday," the most covered song of all time, and also one of the best loved.

McCartney had, in fact, developed two different ballad styles by this point. There were the haunting, almost overwhelmed, songs such as "And I Love Her" and "Here, There and Everywhere," and there were the melancholic tunes, such as "Yesterday" and the superb "For No One." And behind these were the show tunes and standards that the band had begun its career with. Millions of miles from the songs that a contemporary group might start out learning, songs like "Besame Mucho" and "Taste of Honey" gave the Beatles—and McCartney, whose father, Jim, was an old-school musician—an immensely strong grounding in the music of the pre-rock 'n' roll era.

"I Will" comes from that tradition, from its almost calypso style and its reassuring bass (sung rather than played by McCartney, according to some sources), to its somewhat vapid lyric, which harkens back to the bandstand singer tradition. This was to flourish more powerfully (and more annoyingly) on "Honey Pie," but there is still something a little "throw-away" about the song, as though McCartney is merely showing the listener how much he can do with even the smallest amount of effort. In fact, anodyne and empty as "I Will" may be, its technical excellence, almost casual delivery, and utter musical confidence are still striking, and very few groups could come near to pulling it off.

Recorded September 16 at Abbey Road. Overdubbed September 17.

Paul McCartney: lead vocals, bass, acoustic guitar
Ringo Starr: drums, maracas, bongos

Julia

(Credit: Lennon/McCartney. Actual writer: John Lennon)

Without doubt, the pivotal song of John Lennon's career, and indeed his life, "Julia" exists as both a tribute to his late mother and to his new love, Yoko Ono. It is also an emotional "bridge" between the two women, with Lennon saying goodbye to the mother he hardly knew and, as it were, introducing her to the woman who would take her place in his heart.

Lennon's mother, Julia Stanley, was born on March 12, 1914, and married Alfred "Freddie" Lennon during World War II. After John's birth on October 9, 1940, Freddie and Julia separated. Julia's subsequent lifestyle and circumstances made it impossible for her to look after John, who went to live with his Aunt Mimi (Mary Elizabeth Stanley) and her husband George. Mimi took over the mother's role in John Lennon's life for his entire childhood, both before and after George's death.

In the late 1940s, Julia came back into Lennon's life. Mimi had attempted to avoid introducing any further emotional confusion into John's life by keeping Julia away from John, but he found his mother by himself and the two began a new relationship. By all accounts, Julia Lennon was a likeable, breezy person whose relationship with her ten-year-old son was more sisterly than motherly. They shared a similar sense of humor, and Julia's free-spirited nature must have been appealing to her son, who had been brought up fairly rigidly by Mimi. Julia even taught John how to play the banjo. They became very close, and when Lennon was asked by his briefly returned father to choose between his mother and him (Lennon's father was about to return to live in New Zealand), he chose Julia.

On July 15, 1958, Julia Lennon was hit and killed by a car driven by an off-duty policeman. Lennon, now 18 and a fairly rebellious teenager, went berserk, becoming a heavy drinker and violent to men and women. The death of the mother he had been separated from and then reunited with was unbearable for Lennon. When he met Paul McCartney, a man with whom he had virtually nothing in common apart from rock 'n' roll, the fact that McCartney's mother had also died when he was a teenager established a bond between them.

Throughout his Beatles career, married to a woman he had betrayed time and time again, Lennon was deeply unhappy. When he met Yoko Ono and fell overwhelmingly in love with her, his life changed again. One might almost say it started again. Lennon's time with Ono—controversial, rocky, but never dull and always rooted in his love for her—was his happiest. Julia Lennon and Yoko Ono did not always inspire his happiest songs—Julia was the source of the solo songs "Mother" and "My Mummy's Dead," while Ono seems to have inspired more songs about apologizing than anyone in history. Nevertheless, the music he made before his murder that was released as the album *Double Fantasy* was the most relaxed and secure work he had ever committed to record.

In 1968, however, Lennon's life was still in a state of flux. "Julia" was actually demoed before Lennon was divorced, and may well have been written shortly before the recording of the Kinfauns demos (Lennon and Ono had slept together for the first time a week or so before). In its White Album form, it remains as stark and unadorned as it is on the demo tape. It is the only truly "solo" song that Lennon recorded with the Beatles, just himself and an acoustic guitar, and its effect is all the more powerful for that. Lennon's voice comes through clear and not always completely in tune, and the song's nakedness matches its emotional state. Lennon sings both his mother's name and the phrase "ocean child" (Ono's first name in English) in the same line, and it is as if he is merging them together in his mind, effectively transferring his feelings for the one to the other.

Not as lyrically direct as his later work (the songs on his first conventional solo album, *Plastic Ono Band*, would lean much more closely toward the confessional), "Julia" did, however, introduce a new emotional rawness to Lennon's music. Throughout his career, Lennon had been forced to either conceal or alter his work for public consumption. "Help!"—his first attempt at writing a confessional song—was intended by Lennon to be recorded as a slow, emotive tune, but commercial considerations caused it to be recorded as a jaunty up-tempo pop rocker, effectively neutering its honesty in its author's eyes. "Norwegian Wood" began as a song about a failed sexual liaison, but was rewritten to hide the truth from his wife. But from now on, liberated both from convention and from the dictates of what constituted a "Beatles song," Lennon would emphasize the honesty and directness of his music. The same month that the White Album was released, Lennon wrote "Look at Me," the first of the new-style songs to be written that would appear on *Plastic Ono Band*.

Recorded October 13 at Abbey Road. Overdubbed October 17.

John Lennon: lead vocals, acoustic guitar

SIDE THREE

Birthday

(Lennon/McCartney)

The recording sessions for the White Album were rarely full of pleasant occurrences. With band members walking out and people working on their own in corridors, the atmosphere could generally be described as furtive and tense. But on September 18, 1968, the Beatles actually timed a recording session at Abbey Road so they could leave halfway through for a couple of hours to watch television together. The reason for the interrupted session was the first British TV showing of the classic—in fact, arguably the best—1950s rock 'n' roll comedy, *The Girl Can't Help It*.

Twelve years old when it was shown on BBC2 that night, in color for those who had color TVs, *The Girl Can't Help It* is a Frank Tashlin comedy with roots in its producer's animated cartoon days and with a memorable central performance by Jayne Mansfield. The film uses the music industry as a backdrop, and as such features—for the first time in a movie—many of the original rock 'n' roll acts, and in color, too. Gene Vincent, Eddie Cochran, and Little Richard all appeared in the film, and they were all musical heroes of the Beatles. Little Richard, in particular, was McCartney's favorite, as well as an immense musical—and vocal—influence. McCartney sang on the Beatles' covers of Little Richard's "Long Tall Sally" and his version of "Kansas City/Hey Hey Hey," and to this day the great Richard Penniman himself will give you an impression of Paul McCartney learning to sing like Little Richard.

In an era before video and DVD, a film that one actually wanted to see being on TV was a big event. The 1968 screening of *The Girl Can't Help It* was almost certainly the first time any of the Beatles could have seen the film since its original release. By that date, of course, they had met, worked with, and outstripped most of the performers in the movie, but the Beatles were at, heart, rock 'n' roll fans. The screening of a film like this was still an important event to them.

McCartney, before putting out the crisps and the beers, had already worked out the basis of a song in the Little Richard mode, and Lennon added phrases to it later. The final recorded version is a daft and fairly engaging tune, which takes a rise out of the idea of birthday songs. It manages a good deal of enthusiasm in its "we're going to a party party" section, something enhanced by the large crew of backing vocalists. By anyone else's standards, "Birthday" is a fairly awesome rocker. By the Beatles', it's just pretty good.

Paul McCartney has always slightly overestimated the appeal of "Birthday," claiming that it's one of those songs that always gets played at birthday parties. In a perfect world, that would be true.

Recorded September 18 at Abbey Road Studios.

Paul McCartney: lead vocals, piano
John Lennon: lead vocals, lead guitar, backing vocals
George Harrison: bass
Ringo Starr: drums
Yoko Ono: backing vocals
Patti Harrison: backing vocals

Yer Blues

(Credit: Lennon/McCartney. Actual writer: John Lennon)

The British Blues Boom of 1968 was, to many, a wonderful thing. No more would rock music be the cheery idiot child of pop, being cruelly exploited for commercial purposes. Now it would be free to return to its original parent, the blues, and, through the medium of the guitar solo and the heartfelt lyric, be able to express the same pain that the original Delta bluesmen had expressed through their songs, only louder. This, at least, was the idea. Loud, slow, and prone to guitar solos of bedtime-seeking proportions, the blues-influenced rock of the late 1960s was by and large a dull affair, a bloated cul-de-sac that thought taking a sad song and making it louder was a new direction for rock music. The whole thing was summed up by Liverpool poet Adrian Henri in the 1969 song he wrote for his group, the Liverpool Scene: "I've Got Those Fleetwood Mac Chicken Shack John Mayall Can't Fail Blues."

Along the way, admittedly, some great records and some very good bands did emerge. Cream—Eric Clapton's spiky power trio—produced some superb music that took elements of the blues and of contemporary pop and made something new from it. Fleetwood Mac—the early, blues band version, not the coked-up, lace-wearing, freeway elf rock band of the 1970s—had in Peter Green a guitarist whose gorgeous, emotive lines added a strangeness to the band's bluesy pop rock. And over all these bands lay the shadow of Jimi Hendrix, whose then-continuing search for new fusions of rock, pop, and jazz meant that the goalposts for blues rock were always being moved to new and more exciting places.

The Beatles were naturally aware of this new development. As the official kings of rock, they had attended Hendrix's early shows in London (Hendrix had returned the compliment by performing *Sgt Pepper*'s title track at the Isle of Wight festival), and, thanks to George Harrison, they knew Eric Clapton well. They were also aware of new threats. In the mid-1960s, just as Beatlemania was peaking and the clanky, over-grinned sound of Merseybeat was about to be banished into show-tune hell, new, louder, and more aggressive guitar groups, including the Who and the Kinks, were coming to the fore. The Beatles' response was impressive. Neither ignoring them nor copying them, they incorporated the new sounds into their own, melodically stronger music, resulting in the taut riffs of songs such as "Ticket to Ride," "I Feel Fine" (with its then jaw-dropping feedback intro), and "Paperback Writer."

But by 1968, the Beatles had nothing to prove, and in any case had never been much captivated by the blues as a musical form. Never comfortable as a "heavy" band (see "Helter Skelter"), they had also always preferred the speed, wit, and attack of rock 'n' roll to its more ponderous cousin, the blues. Most Beatles tracks with a blues feel are either jokey improvisations, such as Lennon's "Brian Epstein Blues," a vague, comedyless comedy tune about their late manager and his family made up during the White Album sessions, or pointless, unimaginative rambles such as the "legendary" "12 Bar Original," which goes on for days and fails to be original at any point. The Beatles—whose every song relied on invention, surprise, novelty, and impatience with the old— were never going to be a great blues band.

Surprisingly, then, in 1968, Lennon wrote a full-on blues tune, "Yer Blues." More surprisingly, the song—a self-pitying tune full of extremely powerful lyrical imagery—was written during the supposedly blissfully peaceful era of Rishikesh. Interestingly, despite Lennon's later claims to have been writing songs about wanting to die in India, early versions of "Yer Blues" have him feeling "insecure" rather than "suicidal," which is somewhat less dramatic. There is comedy in the song's title—which McCartney suggested to Lennon that he amend, but Lennon admitted he was embarrassed to be so nakedly honest—and lines about eagles and worms may be intended as deliberate exaggerations. Nevertheless, the song is as emotionally direct as anything in Lennon's work. It is the only Beatles song he performed at the Rolling Stones' *Rock 'n' Roll Circus* broadcast in December 1968, and in 1969 at the Toronto Rock 'n' Roll Festival. It is also one of only three Beatles songs he ever performed as a solo artist (the others are his own "Come Together," and McCartney's "I Saw Her Standing There," the latter being sung as a duet with and favor to Elton John).

"Yer Blues" was also intended as a response to the Blues Boom. Its lyrics may veer between send-up and sincerity, but its sound is definitely intended as a challenge, being as loud and rough as possible, and recorded in a small cramped tape room at Abbey Road. In the interests of rawness, one verse—taped into a dead mic—is left vocal-less, and the whole thing sounds like Lennon's attempt to do a "Helter Skelter"; that is, to take on the heavy rock boys at their own game. Sadly, perhaps because of Lennon's own disinterest in the genre he was pastiching, "Yer Blues" is not a great song.

Recorded August 13 at Abbey Road Studios. Overdubbed August 14 and 20.

John Lennon: lead vocals, lead guitar, backing vocals
Paul McCartney: bass
George Harrison: lead guitar
Ringo Starr: drums

Mother Nature's Son

(Credit: Lennon/McCartney. Actual writer: Paul McCartney)

The Rishikesh influence continues. This song is possibly the only Paul McCartney tune ever influenced by a lecture, namely one given by the Maharishi Mahesh Yogi about man's relationship to nature. (The same lecture also inspired Lennon's "Child of Nature." That song's lyrical similarity to "Mother Nature's Son"—and its over-specific lines about "the road to Rishikesh"—must have caused Lennon to drop the song for the White Album and recast it as a tribute to Yoko Ono in the form of "Jealous Guy.")

Something of a brother song to "Blackbird," "Mother Nature's Son" is a beautiful tune, inspired to some extent by the standard "Nature Boy," and shows McCartney in his persona as straw-chewing minstrel. It features one of McCartney's trademark "haunting" melodies, his best wide-eyed tenor vocal, some lovely acoustic plucking, and a nice bit of brass. It was also the scene of a moment of Beatles tension when, as McCartney was supervising the brass overdub with engineer Ken Scott, Lennon and Starr walked in and everything got rather strained, the atmosphere immediately dissipating when they left again. This seems somewhat ironic, given that Lennon was the one who first thought of the idea of the brass overdub in the first place. George Martin had proposed to McCartney that the song needed something to come in near the end, in the manner of music actually seeming to approach the song from a distance, and Lennon had immediately suggested a brass section. Two days after this overdub, Ringo Starr would walk out on the band.

Recorded August 9 at Abbey Road Studios. Overdubbed August 20.

Paul McCartney: lead vocals, acoustic guitar, percussion
Brass

Everybody's Got Something to Hide Except Me and My Monkey

(Credit: Lennon/McCartney. Actual writer: John Lennon)

Once upon a time, Beatle rockers had been simple affairs about men buying diamond rings and women throwing them away. The Chuck Berry tradition was alive and kicking in their music, and everything the Beatles sang about was fun and made sense. By 1968, however, all this had changed. Lennon in particular had abandoned songs like "You Can't Do That" for new horizons. Songs such as "I Am the Walrus" and "Hey Bulldog" altered rock music forever, and did not once mention women or cars in their terrifying lyrics.

Despite being geniuses, the Beatles also had a powerful spine of rock 'n' roll propping them up. This prevented McCartney's sense of whimsy and Lennon's love of randomness and surrealism from getting out of hand during the great psychedelic explosion of 1967. Not for the Beatles would be the worst excesses of Syd Barrett and the teapot tweeness of their contemporaries. The Beatles liked to strap their weirdness to a more powerful frame.

By the time Lennon came to write "Everybody's Got Something to Hide Except Me and My Monkey," psychedelia was waning slightly, waiting to be eventually replaced by the horrors of progressive rock. This song began its life in a slightly different form. As a Kinfauns demo, its chorus and "come on come on"s had more of a lazy, Dylanish feel (the title is itself a classic Bob Dylan pastiche). The verses are very "1967 hippie heaven," with their deliberate lyrical twists and turns and almost meaningless declarations about one's inside being out and one's outside being in. If the song has any meaning, it's about letting it all hang out (almost literally), the importance of honesty (Lennon's new best mate), and the fact that Lennon and Ono are truth-tellers beset by human hypocrisy and so forth. The song also has a strong sexual dimension, and on the demo, the "come on, come on"s are supplemented by Lennon grunting "make it, make it" sotto voce at the end.

On record, the slinkiness of "Everybody's Got Something to Hide" is replaced by a more exciting rock 'n' roll energy. Unlike the similar but stodgier "Birthday," "Everybody's Got Something to Hide" fairly bursts along, all fire bells, chanting, and powerful riff. It is one of the Beatles' more underrated rock songs, perhaps because it doesn't fit the conventional structures of a "Back in the U.S.S.R." and because it's not terribly comprehensible (the reference to a monkey may either be to the "monkey on my back" of heroin addiction parlance or, as Lennon claimed, to Yoko Ono).

Never a hit single for anyone else, the song was done well both by the great Fats Domino and the American new wave group the Feelies, and was also once heard by the author as a Spanish version in a bar in Santander. Efforts to trace this version have proved, sadly, futile. "Everybody's Got Something to Hide Except Me and My Monkey"—which was originally called "Come On, Come On"—has the longest title of any Beatles song.

Recorded in rehearsal June 26 at Abbey Road Studios. Rerecorded June 27. Overdubbed July 1 and 23.

John Lennon: lead vocals, rhythm guitar
Paul McCartney: backing vocals, bass
George Harrison: backing vocals, lead guitar
Ringo Starr: drums

Sexy Sadie

(Credit: Lennon/McCartney. Actual writer: John Lennon)

John Lennon was well known for the misogynist tone of several of his early songs. From "Run for Your Life" to "Norwegian Wood," his work was never particularly pro-women. While this was to change when he met Yoko Ono (and result in a complete turnaround, leading to songs like "Woman Is the Nigger of the World"), he was, easily, the Beatle most likely to write a nasty song about a woman. "Sexy Sadie" therefore, fit neatly into this category. The sensuality of the tune and delivery mirrors Lennon's earlier "Girl," while its threatening message is pure John Lennon.

Fortunately for Lennon's reputation, most of the world

now knows that "Sexy Sadie" is not about a woman at all, but about one of the central characters in the whole White Album story, the Maharishi Mahesh Yogi. The saga of the Maharishi—how he seemingly led the Beatles on, promised them the earth, and then betrayed them with a woman—is one that parallels Lennon's early, untrusting view of womankind and lends itself rather well to the song's narrative.

Returning to London from Rishikesh furious and full of the apparent betrayal, Lennon was moved to write this song as a damning attack on the Maharishi. George Harrison intervened, telling Lennon not to be "ridiculous." (History has subsequently been kinder to the Maharishi than Lennon was; several commentators have since come to the conclusion that the alleged sexual assault was nothing more than some stirring-up done by Beatles leech Alex Mardas.) Consequently, the song mutated into what is actually one of Lennon's more subtly constructed put-down songs. The anger and sarcasm of the original now becomes more sensual. This is, like its lyric, a sexy song, despite the fact that the sensual mood is deliberately undermined by a chord sequence that provokes a sense of unease, followed by out-and-out lyrical threat. The song loses little in its transition from unveiled attack on a world religious leader to knowing put-down of a femme fatale, but is rather let down by a muggy production that buries the subtleties of the arrangement.

As something of a postscript to the whole Rishikesh affair, it's worth noting that, in 1993, George Harrison met the Maharishi again for the first time in 25 years. Harrison and his friend, Deepak Chopra, visited the Maharishi and, according to Chopra, asked the Maharishi for forgiveness, saying by way of explanation, "We were very young." The

Maharishi charmingly replied that the Beatles were angels in disguise. He cited as evidence the famous story of how, apparently, on the night the Beatles appeared on *The Ed Sullivan Show*, for the one hour the show was screened, no crime was reported in the United States. The Maharishi explained that, therefore, there was nothing to forgive. "I could never be upset with angels," he said.

Recorded July 19 at Abbey Road Studios. Rerecorded July 24 and August 13. Overdubbed August 21.

John Lennon: lead vocals, rhythm guitar, acoustic guitar, organ, backing vocals
Paul McCartney: backing vocals, bass, piano
George Harrison: lead guitar, backing vocals
Ringo Starr: drums, tambourine

Helter Skelter

(Credit: Lennon/McCartney. Actual writer: Paul McCartney)
The Beatles, as discussed earlier in this book, were not the kings of maximum heaviosity. Songs like "Yer Blues" did not prove to be convincing as amplified monsters, especially when the likes of Led Zeppelin were emerging on the scene to noisily overwhelm rock music. Unable to compete with this kind of band, the Beatles generally avoided direct rock confrontation and followed their own trails. They always liked a challenge, however, and by 1968 had become increasingly fond of experimentation—which is probably the best way to think about "Helter Skelter."

The song was inspired by McCartney reading an interview

with Pete Townshend, the guitarist and leader of the Who, which, in 1967, was the heaviest band in the world. In the interview, Townshend was talking about a new Who song— almost certainly their single "I Can See for Miles." He claimed it was going to be the loudest and heaviest rock song ever, or some such. (As it happens, while it is one of the greatest rock singles of the 1960s, and is arguably the best song the Who ever released, "I Can See for Miles" is not as heavy as, say, anything by Jimi Hendrix or even Cream.) McCartney, impressed by the concept, decided that anything the Who could do, the Beatles could do better. Accordingly, he set out to write the Heaviest Song In The World.

McCartney was possibly also stung into action by the popular notion that he was the group's Mister Softy and that the real rocker in the band was Lennon. Fuelled by McCartney's authorship of the likes of "Yesterday," this theory ignored the fact that he was the band's best rock 'n' roll singer, and that Lennon had also been responsible for pensive tunes such as "In My Life." In later life, when people made this assertion, McCartney would ask, semi-wryly, "Have you checked?" And "Helter Skelter" is the song that McCartney likes to cite to disprove the Paul Is a Wimp Theory.

A helter skelter is a fairground slide that spirals around a tower-like structure. Taking as his lyrical concept the slightly tongue-in-cheek idea of a helter skelter ride as a metaphor for sex, McCartney put together "Helter Skelter" as a kind of elephantine super-blues. Early versions are extremely long—there is a legendary take of the song that apparently lasts over 25 minutes—and feature the neat semi-rhyme "helter skelter/ hell for leather." Then, one drunken night at Abbey Road, someone decided to speed up the song, and this is the version that ended up on the White Album. It begins fantastically, with a burst of guitar and the chorus manically chattered by McCartney, humps along promisingly on its oddly boinging riff with some stentorian backing vocals, and then . . . it just goes on and on. Neither loud enough to bludgeon the listener into being impressed nor inspired enough to be exciting, "Helter Skelter" rambles along with the odd bit of McCartney exhorting the listener to "look out!" in a fairly vain attempt to keep the excitement going. The song gets a bit dull after two minutes, starts to end after two and half minutes, threatens to end after three, fades out after three and a half, and then comes back again. A paltry four and a half minutes long—no length at all in the epic terms of real heavy rock songs—"Helter Skelter" feels like the whole of Wagner's Ring Cycle compressed into a trilby hat. The song is largely redeemed only by Starr's shout of "I got blisters on my fingers!"

There is a superior version of this song on mono versions of the White Album. It's shorter and snappier, and does not feature a false ending (so 1967, false endings). "Helter Skelter" is also one of the songs that allegedly "inspired" Charles Manson and his Family to go on a murder spree, despite the fact that its lyric is innocuousness itself. Manson's connection with the song in turn inspired cover versions by Siouxsie and the Banshees (see also "Dear Prudence") and the pompous stadium rock group U2, whose singer Bono introduced "Helter Skelter" with the words, "Charles Manson stole this song from the Beatles. We're stealing it back." The Banshees' version is the best of all of them.

Trivia fact: In one of the great moments of White Album history, George Harrison was inspired during these sessions to imitate singer Arthur Brown—then riding high in the charts with "Fire"—by running around the studio with a flaming ashtray on his head.

Recorded July 18 at Abbey Road Studios (25-minute version). Rerecorded September 9. Overdubbed September 10.

Paul McCartney: lead vocals, lead guitar, bass, backing vocals
John Lennon: lead guitar, bass, backing vocals
George Harrison: backing vocals, rhythm guitar
Ringo Starr: drums
Mal Evans: trumpet

Long, Long, Long

(Harrison)

George Harrison was the Spiritual Beatle. Because of this, it has been argued, he is also the one most responsible, in his quiet way, for changing Western society. This is not an outlandish claim. West Coast guru Deepak Chopra—an early intimate of the Maharishi Mahesh Yogi—credits Harrison with single-handedly introducing America to the tenets of Eastern religion, specifically the ideas behind transcendental meditation. Harrison—the first Western popular musician to take Indian music and ideas seriously—had already actively introduced Indian sounds in songs including "Within You, Without You," "Love You To," and "The Inner Light," and he helped to popularize classical Indian music with his sponsorship of Ravi Shankar. Later he would bring solid financial aid to the subcontinent with the Concert for Bangladesh, the 1970s prototype for Live Aid. However, the most important and influential aspect of Harrison's interest in India was his spreading of Eastern spiritual and religious beliefs.

Without going too deeply into the subject, it's clear that the world in the mid-1960s was interested in both questioning old values and investigating new values. Transcendental meditation, Yoga, and Buddhism were new to the West, and were all incorporated into 1960s belief systems. And while previously there had been Western interest in these areas— indeed, the Maharishi himself had something of an international following before 1967—it was the interest of the Beatles that directly sparked the world's infatuation with, and later deeper interest in, Indian beliefs. And the Beatles were led to these ideas solely by George Harrison.

Harrison, who had intended to make a solo visit to Rishikesh but who found himself joined by the other Beatles, was the only member of the band to maintain his interest on a daily basis. Right up to the end of his life, he studied both Indian and Christian religious literature and even on his deathbed was discussing the nature of reincarnation with Deepak Chopra. Famously, when assaulted and nearly murdered, he chanted "Hare Krishna" at his attacker, a sign of his religious faith and his belief in peace over violence.

Always associated with Hare Krishnas and with India, Harrison was the Beatle whose solo career was most mocked and damaged because of his beliefs. While Lennon's political period was a temporary passion (and still produced hit singles), Harrison's religiously inclined solo albums became off-putting to the general listener. "My

Sweet Lord" had engaged the public massively, but by the time songs such as "The Lord Loves the One Who Loves the Lord" were released, interest had waned.

Much of Harrison's best music was inspired by his faith, however, and "Long, Long, Long"—arguably the least fêted of the Beatles' great songs—is no exception to this. A yearning, beautiful song about the happiness that letting God into his life has given Harrison, "Long, Long, Long" is one of Harrison's best songs, and is an oasis of calm and faith in the clattering chaos of the White Album.

Originally called "It's Been a Long, Long, Long Time," this song, with echoing vocals and an eerie ambience that fits the spookiness of some of the best moments of the White Album, is a brief affair. It wafts by in a melancholy fashion until it suddenly breaks into a powerful moment of release, and ends with a moment of serendipity almost too well-known to write about. An empty wine bottle on top of McCartney's Hammond organ starts to wobble, and the players take the sound and enfold it into the song, McCartney playing ghostly chords, Harrison wailing softly, and Starr mimicking the bottle's rattling with his drums. It's a perfect moment in one of the White Album's least known corners.

Recorded October 7 at Abbey Road Studios. Overdubbed October 8 and 9.

George Harrison: lead vocals, acoustic guitar
Paul McCartney: bass, piano, Hammond organ
Ringo Starr: drums

Revolution 1

(Credit: Lennon/McCartney. Actual writer: John Lennon)

"I only like rock 'n' roll," John Lennon once said, and on "Revolution 1," we see the proof. After the electronics and the tape fun of *Sgt. Pepper*, Lennon went on to write a song that owed little or nothing to his previous experimental work (although it would become the basis of a very different musical experiment). Lennon's most famous message song, the one that outraged a generation when its single version was handed over to Nike for a commercial, is also one of his best. So determined was he to promote the song that Lennon made three versions of it. Very few other Beatles songs were remade and remodeled. None was ever reconstructed to the extent that "Revolution" was.

Early versions of the song were written in India, and this is where it's initial unambiguous pacifist tone came from. Still under the influence of the Maharishi, Lennon vaguely thought that the problems of the day would be resolved by love and by God. Always a pacifist by nature, Lennon was also able to see that violence begets violence and that taking on the "pigs" at their own game would only make things worse. He said the song's message was "don't aggravate the pig by waving a red flag in his face." Lennon was also suspicious of professional activists such as Jerry Rubin and Abbie Hoffman. Echoing the song's lyric, he later claimed that when talking politics and revolution with these people, he always wanted to "see the plan."

"Revolution" also charts Lennon's journey from spiritual hippie to Dadaist bed-in protester to Maoist sympathizer, and was to be the yardstick by which his political commitment would be measured, both by him and by his left-wing critics. It is Lennon's first confrontational song (the "you" and "I" of the lyric are no longer boyfriend and girlfriend, but two activists engaged in fairly sparky political debate), his first manifesto song, and one of the first of Lennon's songs to completely abandon metaphor for direct, unambiguous imagery. Throughout the early 1970s, songs such as "Working Class Hero," "Power to the People," and the unpopular and often ludicrous "Some Time in New York City" would see Lennon position himself as a left-wing activist, interested in using songs as vehicles for important messages. Of this era's songs, only the timeless "Happy Xmas (War Is Over)" has survived with any dignity.

In 1968, Lennon was still a couple of years away from wearing Mao badges, dressing in combat gear, and not wanting to see the plan. "Revolution" was still an ambiguous song. On both vocal versions he would vacillate on the "you can count me out/in/out" sections, uncertain himself how he felt about fighting the Man on the barricades. But the song was still too political for the other Beatles, who objected to Lennon's insistence that "Revolution" be the band's next single.

Lennon was happy with the song. As students fought the police in Paris, as the antiwar movement grew in strength, and as radical politics replaced hippie nonviolent protest, he felt that he should say something about the situation. On "Revolution" he felt that he had, and was angry and disappointed when McCartney, ever the diplomat, said the song was too slow to be a single (which is fair enough). So Lennon rerecorded "Revolution" as a fast song, the blasting rocker that became the flipside of "Hey Jude."

The version of "Revolution" on the White Album is of course the first one: its lazy groove and fat-cow-like brass do make the song somewhat complacent and sedentary. This impression is further enhanced by the doo-wop backing vocals, which seem intended to reassure the hot-headed revolutionary listener. Despite Lennon's superbly reasoned and even witty lyric, only his almost muttered "in" after "count me out" gives the song any bite.

This version is notable for being one of the most conventional pieces of music the Beatles ever recorded. It was also, paradoxically, the springboard for experimentalism. In addition to Lennon's attempts to vary his vocal style (even lying on his back to sing at one point), the band originally continued to play for some ten minutes after the end of the song on record. Lennon kept the extra minutes as the basis of what would become "Revolution 9." (Along the way, another version was put together as well, with McCartney and Harrison singing what has become known as the "mama papa mama papa" backing vocal.)

"Revolution 1"'s fame comes largely from its remade version, whose attack matched its title better, and whose lyric, duplicated entirely from the White Album version, was to inspire political debate for several years. Lennon was always brought back to it, largely to be chastised for not being left-wing enough, and, on "Power to the People," would even quote it himself.

The song was the direct basis of an answer song by Nina Simone, also called "Revolution." This song was critical of Lennon's comparatively apolitical stance, and Lennon apparently liked it. "Revolution" also inspired the Beach Boys' rather daft remake of "Riot in Cell Block 9, Student Demonstration Time," which is quite rocky, but did nothing for the band's reputation as political sages.

Recorded May 30 at Abbey Road Studios. Overdubbed May 31, June 4, and June 21.

John Lennon: lead vocals, guitar, backing vocals
Paul McCartney: bass, organ
George Harrison: backing vocals
Ringo Starr: drums
Brass

Honey Pie

(Credit: Lennon/McCartney. Actual writer: Paul McCartney)

Bowing out on a rather hokey note, Paul McCartney effectively leaves the White Album after this song (save for his appearance on the "Can You Take Me Back?" fragment that's heard just before "Revolution 9"). "Honey Pie"'s bizarre lyric about McCartney's being too lazy to visit America to see his newly famous girlfriend is so unambiguous that only a madman could misinterpret it. And so Charles Manson did, seeing "Honey Pie" as an invitation to travel to London to meet the Beatles.

In the realm of the sane, "Honey Pie"—a song inspired by McCartney's love of the dance bands his father used to play with—offers up McCartney as the master pasticheur in action again. This time he presents a tune that is so perfect a parody that it could actually have appeared in a Fred Astaire film, were it not so smug. The song is brilliantly constructed, right down to the scratchy 78 rpm record effect on the line

"Now she's hit the big time" (needless to say, all vocal and musical effects were in place on the demo, which is very much a Paul McCartney trademark). John Lennon—who would later laugh at the song—even contributes an immaculate Django Reinhardt pastiche guitar break (much to George Harrison's admiration). Despite all of this, "Honey Pie" is a charming song that outstays its welcome on about the third or fourth hearing. Its sole purpose seems to be to demonstrate how adept McCartney is at absorbing musical styles, something he was always eager to prove.

Even in the Hamburg days, McCartney was experimenting with different idioms. Bizarre as it may seem, the delightful "When I'm 64"—the best pastiche song the Beatles ever wrote—was written in the crazed speed chaos of the Hamburg Star-Club, and was even part of their stage show (presumably not the part where John Lennon wore a toilet seat around his neck and shouted "Shitty shitty!" at German sailors). Once that song was unleashed on *Sgt. Pepper*, and its popularity was proven (the author can remember an episode of anodyne Christian pop star Cliff Richard's TV show, in which he engaged in the ritual slaughter of "When I'm 64"), McCartney was free to indulge his penchant for granny-pleasers. Indeed, his next song in the nostalgia idiom, "Your Mother Should Know," sounds like a direct appeal to the over-65s, and only fails in its mission by not being a song that anybody's mother would want to get up and dance to.

After his final trip to vaudeville with the Beatles on the band-loathed "Maxwell's Silver Hammer," McCartney continued to indulge his Tin Pan Alley bent throughout his solo years. From "Uncle Albert/Admiral Halsey" and "You

Gave Me the Answer" to, arguably, "We All Stand Together" and "Mull of Kintyre," his desire to "prove himself" as a talented all-rounder (when the world already knows that no more gifted songwriter has ever lived) has made McCartney a frustrating individual. However, his diversions into music hall and light entertainment serve only to highlight the brilliance of the rest of his work.

At least, that's the kind of thing to try and keep in mind when listening to "Honey Pie" for the fortieth time.

Recorded October 1 at Trident Studios. Overdubbed October 2 and 4.

Paul McCartney: lead vocals, piano
John Lennon: lead guitar
George Harrison: bass, backing vocals
Ringo Starr: drums
Brass

Savoy Truffle

(Harrison)

The songwriter's art is a varied one. One minute, he or she may be setting the world to rights, the next, writing a song about . . . Eric Clapton's teeth. "Savoy Truffle"—the fourth of the diffuse quartet of songs that George Harrison contributes to the White Album—took its lyrical inspiration from a box of chocolates. "At that time he [Clapton] had a lot of cavities in his teeth and needed dental work," Harrison recalled later. "He always had a toothache but he ate a lot of chocolates . . . and once he saw a box he had to eat them all."

Harrison, seeking inspiration from the written word, derived a good chunk of the lyric to "Savoy Truffle" from the names of the chocolates that Clapton was working his way through even as Harrison was writing. Thanks to the efforts of Beatle obsessives, we know now that the particular brand of chocolates with which Eric Clapton was ruining his already fragile teeth were Mackintosh's Good News Double Centre Chocolate Assortment. (George was forced to make up a couple of chocolate names to pad out the lyric.)

The song's "message" is that "you are what you eat." Harrison was given this idea by Derek Taylor, who took it from the title of a short film made by Taylor's friend, Alan Pariser. Harrison also sings, "We all know Ob-La-Di, La-Da," which, given the amount of time the band had spent on that song, may be an exhausted statement of fact (or, more likely, just some nonsense).

The track itself—compressed to the point of constipation—is something of a pop rocker. It has a nice sheen to it (its use of a brass section is something that Harrison would continue to develop in his solo work). Most intriguing, however, is the tone of an oddly Lennonesque snarl to the whole thing.

Recorded October 3 at Trident Studios. Overdubbed October 5, 11, and 14.

George Harrison: lead vocals, lead guitar
Paul McCartney: bass
Ringo Starr: drums, tambourine
Chris Thomas: organ, electric piano
Brass

Cry Baby Cry

(Credit: Lennon/McCartney. Actual writer: John Lennon)

The first of the songs to be demoed at Kinfauns, "Cry Baby Cry" is a fantastic song. Its author disagreed rather strongly—he called it "a piece of rubbish." This has always baffled Beatles fans, who see it as a fine and slightly creepy song, in many ways the centerpiece of the "spooky" White Album songs.

The song's lyric was inspired by several sources. One was a TV ad on at the time that apparently declared "Cry baby cry, make your mother buy." Another was the children's nursery rhyme "Sing a Song of Sixpence" (its reference to blackbirds may have brought it back into Lennon's mind after hearing McCartney work on "Blackbird"). The third source was Lewis Carroll's *Alice in Wonderland*.

Lennon was a great lover of Lewis Carroll, whose blend of comic surrealism and dreamlike imagery very much appealed to him. Lennon had already appropriated the figure of the Walrus from Carroll's poem "The Walrus and the Carpenter" for "I Am the Walrus" (believing Carroll's Walrus to be the "good guy," Lennon was quite upset to discover that he had in fact aligned himself with an evil, lying oyster-snaffler. This may be the real reason that he wrote "Glass Onion" and told the world that the walrus was Paul).

"Cry Baby Cry," with its eerie cast of fairytale nobility engaged in bizarrely mundane domestic tasks, its references to seances in the dark, and its constant references to a group of unseen children, is a song with an air of a particularly dreamlike ghost story. Lennon's delivery—dry, neutral, almost not there—adds a lot to the song's peculiar ambience. It is one of the strangest and most beautiful lyrics on the White Album.

While one can see that Lennon—rejecting his lyrical past and his fondness for the obscure but effective lyric—might have dismissed the song for not being about anything concrete, it is clear that he was, for once, wrong about his own work.

Recorded July 15 and 16 Abbey Road Studios. Overdubbed July 18.

John Lennon: lead vocals, acoustic guitar, piano, organ
Paul McCartney: bass
George Harrison: lead guitar
Ringo Starr: drums
George Martin: harmonium

Can You Take Me Back?

(Not credited. Actual writer: Paul McCartney)

Recorded, and quite probably improvised, at the end of take 19 of "I Will" (along with a version of "Step Inside Love," a song McCartney wrote for Cilla Black, and "Los Paranoias," a parody of the South American-styled group Los Paraguayos), "Can You Take Me Back?" is a fragment of song that displays McCartney's gift for the miniature and his beautifully simple craftsmanship. The song is not listed on the album's sleeve notes, and its position at the start of "Revolution 9" adds to that song's sense of imminent danger and slight menace. While brief, "Can You Take Me Back?" is a true hidden treasure of the White Album.

Paul McCartney: lead vocals, bass
John Lennon: backing vocals

George Harrison: acoustic guitar, backing vocals
Ringo Starr: drums

Revolution 9

(Credit: Lennon/McCartney. Actual writers: John Lennon/Yoko Ono/George Harrison)

One of the most exciting recordings ever made (or, if you are dull, eight minutes of squawking), "Revolution 9" is still, after nearly a quarter of a century, the most radical and innovative track ever to bring a rock record to its climax. The song's placing on a conventional pop record is daring, much more so than if it had been a side "art" project for the Beatles (no one discusses George Harrison's *Electronic Sounds* solo album much, because almost no one has ever heard it).

As anyone who has ever found the White Album on a CD jukebox will know, "Revolution 9" is literally subversive, an avant-garde recording that can be found in millions of houses, apartments, wine bars, and other settings where people hoping to relax to a bit of "Ob-La-Di, Ob-La-Da" suddenly find themselves subjected to nearly ten minutes of backward-recorded tape and the cacophony of rioting crowds, Northerners reciting lists of dances, and Yoko Ono informing the world that one becomes naked. No one in the history of recorded music has ever been so successful in introducing such extreme music to so many people, most of whom, admittedly, will try their best never to hear "Revolution 9." Those who do listen to it usually find that it not only rewards repeated playing (and causes adults to walk around their homes chanting "they'd get a little bit older and a little bit slower"), but that it also knocks other tracks on the White Album into a cocked hat. "Revolution 9," for all its lack of melody, its length, its chaos, and its refusal to be lovable mop-top music, is one of the best things the Beatles ever did.

It was hugely influenced, of course, by the presence of Yoko Ono. Ono had worked on sound pieces as a member of the Fluxus group, and she was a vital part of the New York avant-garde. Lennon had enjoyed tape experiments in the past, and had dabbled in aspects of audio verité (the burst of a radio production of *King Lear* toward the end of "I Am the Walrus," the spliced-up tapes of fairground organs on "Being for the Benefit of Mister Kite," and so on). He was instantly drawn to any new idea, particularly, one suspects, anything that would make his more conventional collaborators George Martin and Paul McCartney nervous. (In fact, however, Martin has always gone out of his way to state his admiration for "Revolution 9," calling it "the music of the future.")

Having already vetoed the release of the infinitely more conventional "Revolution 1" as a single, thereby provoking the recording of the proto-punk "Revolution," McCartney was understandably not keen to give over nearly ten minutes of the new Beatles album to a collage of tape loops, sound effects, and Yoko Ono. He and the other Beatles tried to get Lennon to leave the piece off the album, with no success.

McCartney was in New York when Lennon, Ono, and Harrison put together "Revolution 9." (Later he would mention his absence from this recording whenever someone brought up Lennon's griping about not being asked to appear on "Why Don't We Do It in the Road?") His input would have been interesting, as he was previously regarded as the Avant-Garde Beatle, putting together the piece of music known as "Carnival of Light," a fourteen-minute cacophony designed for a London happening at the Chalk Farm Roundhouse. McCartney had also expressed an interest in the work of Karl-Heinz Stockhausen, the king of classical avant-garde. McCartney has, in recent years, made efforts to change the public's image of him as the cozy, domestic Beatle and of Lennon as the great radical experimenter. He has a point. On the other hand, he didn't make "Revolution 9."

The construction of the piece—its hours of tape looping involved lots of people holding pencils to keep the loops up—was laborious. Ono supervised the session with Lennon, and made choices about which sections to use. Lennon had compiled a battery of classical music edits, spoken word sections, and a Royal Academy of Music audition tape on which a nameless, well-spoken man said the words "number nine, number nine, number nine." These were all laid over the final section of "Revolution 1," which vanishes under the weight of the new loops, and edited together to produce the powerful melange that now appears on the White Album.

The number nine was significant for Lennon. He was fascinated by the number, naming the song "Number Nine Dream" after it, and seemed to feel it had some mystic significance for him. He was born on October 9, 1940 (and had his son Sean's birth induced so that Sean could be born on October 9, 1975). Brian Epstein saw the Beatles on November 9, 1962, and they were signed on May 9, 1962. And so forth.

The point of the track, Lennon said, was to describe what he thought the sound of revolution would be like. Later he reversed this opinion (largely because he was talking to left-wing activists and wanted to look good) and said the piece was antirevolution; that is, that it presented revolution in a bad light and hinted that said revolution might be chaotic, violent, and negative. Whatever Lennon's view was, it does not change the fact that "Revolution 9" is an extremely effective sound collage.

It has many high points. Over some gently mocking piano, it begins with Beatles' press officer Derek Taylor apologizing to George Martin for not having brought him a bottle of Chablis. It features Lennon and Harrison running through a list of early 1960s dances, most notably the Twist and the Watusi. There is the "number nine" loop, surely one of the most calmly sinister effects on any pop record. Bits of orchestral music come in— the final chord of Sibelius' Symphony No. 7, a bit of Beethoven's Opus 80. Lennon shouts "Hold it!," an American football crowd roars "Block that kick!," and Lennon intones, "Take this, brother, may it serve you well." Finally, as the piece fades, Ono can be heard musing, "You become naked . . ." The whole thing is quite extraordinary and is without doubt a high point of the Beatles' career.

"Revolution 9" is the longest track ever to be released under the name of the Beatles. For some strange reason, it has never been included in any compilation release or released as a single.

Recorded May 30 at Abbey Road Studios. Effects added June 6, 10, 11, 20, and 21.

John Lennon: tape loops, spoken vocals
George Harrison: spoken vocals
Yoko Ono: tape loops, spoken vocals

Good Night

(Credit: Lennon/McCartney. Actual writer: John Lennon)

What better way to follow an eight-minute aural collage of chaos and disruption than with a lullaby sung by Ringo Starr, accompanied by an orchestra and the massed might of the Mike Sammes Singers? The fact that both "Revolution 9" and "Good Night" are John Lennon compositions says everything about his versatility, not to mention his sense of humor.

"Good Night" was written by Lennon as a lullaby for his five-year-old son Julian. He later described the song as "possibly overlush," but this is part of its appeal. Lennon asked George Martin, one of the most restrained producers and orchestral arrangers in popular music, to give "Good Night" a real "Hollywood" feel. Martin obliged magnificently, with strings that sweep Ringo up a twinkling glass staircase onto a fairytale balcony. Starr returned the favor with his most lugubrious crooning vocal on a Beatles record to date. Never the ironist, Ringo was cast perfectly on this song, and was able to sing a potentially super-cheesy lyric with genuine gentleness and sincerity.

Many listeners have been surprised to learn that "Good Night" was written by Lennon (and several commentators have simply assumed that it was one of McCartney's— although, in truth, McCartney would never be quite as gloopy or as saccharine as Lennon is here). At the time, Ringo said "It was John who wrote it for me. He's got a lot of soul, John has."

For his part, McCartney always felt that, by giving the song to Ringo, Lennon was hiding his own emotions and protecting his tough-guy reputation. Certainly Lennon's relationship with Julian was not a perfect one. Usually either away on tour or home on drugs, Lennon left Julian's mother Cynthia when Julian was five, and, living in New York, was a fairly absent parent. Given that the plight of young Julian at the time of the Lennon divorce inspired McCartney's astonishing "Hey Jude"—and also that, later, Lennon was to write the super-sweet but openly loving "Beautiful Boy" for his second son, Sean Ono Lennon—"Good Night" is not one of the great emotional father/son songs.

The song originally had a spoken introduction, in which Starr instructed his youthful listeners to toddle off to bed. "Good Night" concludes the White Album in classic Beatles fashion, both as a perfect and logical ending and, because of its placing after "Revolution 9" and its epic lushness, as something of a surprise finish, too.

Recorded June 28 at Abbey Road Studios. Overdubbed July 2. Remade July 22.

Ringo Starr: lead vocals
Mike Sammes Singers: backing vocals
Orchestra

THE ONES THAT GOT AWAY: THE SONGS THAT FELL OFF THE WHITE ALBUM

Even at 30 songs long, there wasn't room on the White Album for everything the Beatles wrote, demoed, and even recorded for it. Some songs weren't good enough, some didn't quite work out, some were just waiting for their moment, and one of them was so horrible that no one ever wants to hear it again. These seven songs—one can presume that the unpleasant and silly "Brian Epstein Blues" was never intended for public consumption—are the ones known to have been slated for inclusion on the White Album.

What's the New Mary Jane?

(Lennon)

Supposed by some to have been partly the work of "Magic" Alex Mardas, alleged inventor and probable source of malicious Maharishi gossip, "What's the New Mary Jane?" is a truly horrible piece of music. Over a backing track of bells and minimalist piano, Lennon sings a pleasantly childlike list of Mary Jane's attributes, which include being "married to Yeti" and having a contract with Apple—and then goes into one of the most annoying choruses of all time. "What a shame Mary Jane had a pain at the party," he sings over and over again, until you want to wrest the CD from its drawer and shove it into a blender.

Despite its awfulness, "What's the New Mary Jane?" (its title is presumably some sort of awful pun on the word marijuana) has had a long and exciting life. It went through the whole Kinfauns-to-studio process like a real song and was apparently actually proposed as a single at one or two points in the Beatles' final days. This dismal song eventually came to rest on the third of the Beatles' *Anthology* discs, where innocent people who have done nothing wrong can hear it.

Child of Nature

(Lennon)

A beautiful, lazy vocal in Lennon's best 1968 style glides like a tipsy dragonfly over some mandolin-type guitar to produce an aptly Eastern effect. "Child of Nature" is a companion piece of sorts to McCartney's "Mother Nature's Son," both songs being based on a Maharishi lecture. McCartney's song aims for a more robust feel—his "Mother Nature's Son," a "poor young country boy," sounds more like a farm boy than anything else. Lennon goes for the more ethereal, and is somewhat specific in his lyrical thrust (the song begins with the words "On the road to Rishikesh"). Perhaps because of this, and probably because of Lennon's disillusionment with the Maharishi, the song was discarded. It reemerged with a different lyric as "Jealous Guy" on the *Imagine* album and became a rock classic.

Junk

(McCartney)

Another extremely resilient outtake, "Junk" (also known in its early versions as "Jubilee") is a wafting tune with a delightful McCartney lyric about, well, junk—a bittersweet lament for all things lost and passed. It would have been a fine song with which to end one of the White Album's four sides, and its theme would have fitted the original *Doll's House* concept extremely well. As it was, the song was held over through the recording of both *Let It Be* and *Abbey Road*, and surfaced, along with "Teddy Boy," another Beatles reject, on McCartney's first solo album in 1970 (where it was joined by an instrumental version, "Singalong Junk"). Since then, it has turned up on the odd film soundtrack and, most notably, the 1990s McCartney solo live album, *Unplugged*.

Etcetera

(McCartney)

The most mysterious Beatles song of them all, "Etcetera" was demoed by McCartney at Abbey Road on August 20, 1968, and then taken home by him. It has never appeared on any record, including bootlegs. It's quite possible that it actually never existed as a song, or that "Etcetera" was a working title for a later song. (The Beatles were famous for giving songs names like "Laxton's Superb," "This Is Some Friendly," and "Scrambled Eggs" when their real names were, respectively, "I Want to Tell You," "Don't Pass Me By," and "Yesterday.") Either way, its title exists today to tantalize those fans who believe that, somewhere out there, a great lost Beatles song is waiting to be discovered.

Sour Milk Sea

(Harrison)

This song was eventually given to Jackie Lomax, a recent Apple signing on whose album all of the Beatles (except Lennon) played. Lomax was the singer with one of the original Merseybeat bands (i.e., the R & B rockers, not the crappy Beatles rip-off ones), called the Undertakers, whose advance to the top of the charts was marred, some feel, by their deeply morbid image.

"Sour Milk Sea" is, like many Harrison songs, quite didactic, but it has a positive thrust, advising listeners to get out of said sour milk sea and live their lives. It's also, even in the Kinfauns demo version, a belting number, with a superb wailing Harrison vocal and a nice twisty melody that's a superior cousin to "Savoy Truffle." At the time, even the super-critical-of-other-people's-songs McCartney opined that the song "could be a rocker." It's clear that, had the song been written by anyone other than a Beatle, it would be fêted by rock critics as a psychedelic classic.

Circles

(Harrison)

Over a backing of creepy organ chords and with a breathy vocal, Harrison sings about the circular nature of life. The results are entertaining and slightly eerie, but the song's faint (and certainly unintentional) resemblance to the feel of Lennon's "Julia," as well as its slightly unworked-out nature were to sideline "Circles" for over a decade. It would eventually appear on a Harrison solo album (*Gone Troppo* in 1982) in acoustic form.

Not Guilty

(Harrison)

Famously recorded in 110 takes, "Not Guilty" was a great lost Beatles song until the release of the third volume of the Beatles' *Anthology*. There are, however, many different versions of this song knocking about (well, there would be, with 110 takes). Aimed at an unnamed adversary, "Not Guilty" is in some ways a sister song to Harrison's

"Wah-Wah" (which turned up on *All Things Must Pass*, and which is about McCartney and the final vexing days of the Beatles). The line in "Not Guilty" about not leading someone astray on the road to Marrakesh may be an allusion to the trip to Rishikesh, which Harrison had planned to take alone until the rest of the band decided they wanted to come along.

the design

"Pop Art should be popular, transient, expendable,
low-cost, mass-produced, young, witty, sexy, gimmicky,
glamorous, and big business."

Richard Hamilton, White Album sleeve designer

THE BEATLES HAD PIONEERED ALBUM DESIGN throughout their
career, from the half-silhouetted headshots of *With the Beatles*
(entitled *Meet the Beatles* in the United States) which became
one of the most imitated sleeves of the 1960s, to the band
name-omitting cover for *Rubber Soul*. In 1967, they had taken
album design into a new area by commissioning pop artist
Peter Blake to put together the sleeve of *Sgt. Pepper's Lonely
Hearts Club Band*. Blake's sleeve was, appropriately for such an
extravaganza of an album, a lush collection of Edwardian
imagery, rich bright colors, pop imagery, and even a selection
of cut-out-and-keep memorabilia. (The inner sleeve, on the
other hand, was by the useless Dutch artist collective The
Fool and looks like rubbish.)

Seeking to continue this tradition with the White Album,
the Beatles went to another fine artist. This time, on the advice
of McCartney's friend Robert Fraser, they hired Richard
Hamilton. Hamilton's rock 'n' roll credentials were excellent.
In 1967, he had made an etching called *Swingeing London* [sic],
which was based on a photograph of Robert Fraser and Mick
Jagger being arrested on drug charges and handcuffed.

Born in 1922 in London, Richard Hamilton studied art at
a variety of art schools, including the classic school for art

rockers, St. Martin's. After the war and national service, he founded the Independent Group of artists with Eduardo Paolozzi, who had taught the late Stuart Sutcliffe, the Beatles' first bass player and a talented artist.

In 1956, Hamilton made his first foray into pop art with a collage for an exhibition called *This Is Tomorrow* (a title later nicked by one of Hamilton's ex-pupils, Bryan Ferry, for a song).

Hamilton was, essentially, the inventor of British pop art. His famous piece *Just What Is It That Makes Today's Homes So Different, So Appealing?*—described by Hamilton as his "personal manifesto"—is one of the most important and influential pieces of postwar British art. Hamilton also has a sense of humor—one of his 1962 pieces is entitled *Towards a Definitive Statement on the Coming Trends in Men's Wear and Accessories.* "There's no reason why art shouldn't be amusing," he once said. "I like the idea of there being a certain hilarity possible in art."

This same sense of humor led Hamilton to follow up the sleeve for *Sgt. Pepper*—that blast of color, detail, and excitement—with its polar opposite, a blank white square. (Certainly, his other idea of placing a round brown mark on the white sleeve, as if made by a coffee cup, was not entirely serious.) The Beatles, by Hamilton's own account, liked the white idea (they thought the stain idea was "a bit too flippant"). They also enjoyed the humor of Hamilton's third suggestion. He proposed that the record have a serial number printed on each copy, to make it look like a limited edition. This was an ironic idea, given that the "limited edition" of the first pressing of the White Album would run to several million copies.

Hamilton also asked the Beatles if they had ever released an album called just "The Beatles." They never had. So the album became *The Beatles*. Its sleeve color and lack of title have of course meant that no one on earth has ever referred to *The Beatles* as anything other than "the White Album."

To leaven the arctic wasteland of the design, Hamilton included four extremely high-quality photographs of the individual Beatles. Of the four shots, McCartney is notably nearer the lens and more doe-eyed than ever, while Lennon appears to be the scruffiest, as though he is preparing to become a spokesman for the people. Hamilton also put together a design for an enormous poster, which would be a lyric sheet on one side of the paper and a collage of Beatles pictures on the other. Each Beatle handed over childhood photos, early Beatles shots, posters, programs, and drawings, and Hamilton put these together. The result—which goes through every aspect of the band's career—is powerful and dramatic, a random-looking but beautifully put together run-through of the Beatles' decade of power. There are Hamburg rocker shots, silly Fabs poses, a picture of them with the prime minister, a shot of McCartney in the bath, and a Lennon drawing. (The last two were censored in South Africa, but at that time, what wasn't?)

Hamilton worked very hard on the collage, spending days sifting through photographs to see what worked best. He even engineered the poster so that it worked visually when folded into quarters, which is how it arrived in the sleeve of the vinyl album. "Its standards are those of a small limited edition print—pushed, with only some technical constraints, to an edition of millions," he wrote later.

The Beatles was released in November 1968, and early pressings do have Hamilton's limited edition numbering (this idea was later revived for the 30th anniversary CD). The design has always been popular, although some commentators have questioned its aptness for such a varied, attic-like album. In fact, the album's very blankness means that, for once, the sleeve does not lead the listener to make assumptions about the contents. Also, it just looks fantastic.

other music of 1968

"The Beatles saved the world from boredom."

George Harrison

THE YEAR OF THE WHITE ALBUM was, like any other year in popular music, a mixture of sudden shifts and peculiar bouts of uneventfulness. For many years, the Beatles' position in pop was a simple one. After 1962, they were not "in" pop music at all, but hovering somewhere above it. (There is even a school of thought that says the Beatles destroyed popular music, crushing with their overwhelming talent millions of genres and millions of lesser talents.) But by 1968, their complete and utter dominance over pop music was finally waning. Having been asked since they formed (it had even become a band in-joke) when "the bubble would burst," the Beatles were prepared for this, to say the least, and would soon be glad of it. But in 1968, they found a harsher music world—one capable not only of doing some things better than them, but even of doing without them. Commercially, of course, things were fine. The chart glitch caused by "Penny Lane/Strawberry Fields Forever" not making the number one spot had been erased in the public mind after the world-crunching demolition of all other artists, and indeed forms of music, that was *Sgt. Pepper*'s success. Artistically, however, the world was a different place.

Before 1968, the Beatles had led pop in hundreds of different ways. They were the first British act to be taken seriously as a rock—or even pop—group around the world.

They were the first hugely successful act to write all their own songs—when their third album, *A Hard Day's Night*, was released, it was noted with some incredulity that all the songs on it were written by the group. They moved from genre to genre with incredible ease, they virtually invented the idea of the studio band, and, with George Martin, they moved the boundaries of what could be done in a studio into outer space. They were so popular and so influential that when they sang, "With our love we could change the world," people believed them.

But by 1968, their various dalliances with drugs, beards, and gurus meant that the Beatles were finally seen as mortal. Other acts, who still looked up to them, were also finally able to breathe some of their own air. Most notably, the Beatles were not a great rock band. While they had been able to take on the new psychedelic acts such as Pink Floyd at their own game, they would find it increasingly hard to challenge the new amplified guitar bands. Always more imaginative and melodic than the rockers, the Beatles simply did not have it in them to crush and destroy. They were not metal.

1968 was the year that, thanks partly to bands like the Beatles, albums rather than singles started to be seen as the true "art form" of rock music. Once albums had been derided as merely a way of padding out a collection of pop singles. Now they were seen as the purest form of rock expression. 1968 was the first year that sales of albums were greater than those of singles in the United Kingdom.

1968 was also a tougher year than 1967. Violence and politics replaced peace and love, and music inevitably reflected that. If 1967 was the year of the kaftan, then 1968 was the year of the RAF greatcoat. In terms of the actual music being made, 1968—a year already dominated by new rock acts including Cream and Jimi Hendrix—was the year that Jimmy Page formed the New Yardbirds, who were soon to change their name to Led Zeppelin. The New Yardbirds toured and recorded and soon perfected the extraordinary mixture of over-amplified rock and elongated blues that was to be the most influential white music of the next ten years. In January 1969, the month the Beatles began to record *Let It Be*, Led Zeppelin released its debut album.

That same year, the seeds of other kinds of rock were sewn. Progressive rock was being born. On one side, the departure of the acid-ruined Syd Barrett from Pink Floyd meant that the band was forced to rethink its future, and its jamming-based rock noodlings would change rock again. The Beatles, being merely gifted at writing songs, would not stand a chance in this world.

Meanwhile, rock continued to harden. the Rolling Stones finally gave up on years of following in the Beatles' musical footsteps. (Lennon later said that anything the Beatles did, the Stones would do six months later.) With the fiasco of the *Pepper*-esque enormity that was *Their Satanic Majesties Request*, the Stones became a full-on dirty blues rock band. In 1968, they released "Jumping Jack Flash," a single that introduced what would effectively be the band's sound for the next 20 years. The same year saw the Rolling Stones bring out *Beggars Banquet*, an album that contained "Street Fighting Man," a far less ambiguous (and sillier) song than Lennon's "Revolution." (That album was also notable for the even more absurd "Sympathy for the Devil," a song whose lyric would have appalling repercussions for the band a year later at the Altamont rock festival.) Meanwhile, the utterly unpretentious (unless pretending to be a truck driver is pretentious) Creedence Clearwater Revival was having hits with short, direct, and seemingly simple three-minute singles such as "Suzie Q," bringing back the rock 'n' roll that records like *Sgt. Pepper* had moved away from. (At the same time, the charts were full of reissue hits from original rock 'n' rollers such as Bill Haley and the late Buddy Holly.)

The Band—who had worked with Bob Dylan for years as the Hawks—reemerged with beards and a look of men who had lived too long in frontier shacks about them. Their first album, *The Band*, and their debut single, "The Weight," introduced a kind of rock music that was at once familiar and baffling, old and new. Dylan himself was pursuing a new, simpler direction with the bleak, folky *John Wesley Harding* album. A year before the Beatles decided that a return to their musical origins was in order, rock was discovering all kinds of roots it never knew it had.

Even Elvis Presley was getting back to his roots. By 1968, Elvis was something of a joke in hip circles. His early work invented rock music for most of his listeners, who included the young Lennon and McCartney. After his army service, however, he seemed castrated (Lennon later famously remarked that Elvis died when he went into the army). In the mid-1960s, Presley seemed incapable of doing anything other than making feeble movies that only humorless kitsch fans find endearing today. His return to TV for the first time in almost a decade looked far from promising. Aired in the United States on December 3, 1968, the show was intended by Presley's manager, Colonel Tom Parker—all three of whose names were assumed—to be a hokey crapfest of Tin Pan Alley nonsense. Instead, the show's producer, Steve Binder, managed to turn it into a reminder of Elvis's early rock 'n' roll brilliance and proof that Presley was still some kind of sexual nuclear bomb. Elvis, "starved to perfection" as famous biographer and baddie Albert Goldman once put it, frugged and yowled like living intercourse in the best leather outfit ever made. The *1968 Comeback Special*, as millions know it today, was an extraordinary turnaround for Elvis, and one more example of a new spirit of rock renewal in the air. That spirit benefited Presley, Dylan, the Rolling Stones, and other barons of the new rock aristocracy, but as the events of 1969 were to show, it came too late to save the Beatles.

Roots rock apart, 1968 was a confusing year. The show *Hair* came out on Broadway, inventing the rock musical. (Unlike the rock opera, the rock musical is written and performed by people who are generally not rock performers at all.) Louis Armstrong recorded "What a Wonderful World." And, best of all (if you disliked Cream and Pink Floyd), bubblegum was the teen/kiddie music of the day, with hundreds of ridiculous, childish, and catchy songs all called "Yummy Yummy Yummy" and "Simon Says," and all recorded by bands with names like the 1910 Fruitgum Company. Otis Redding had a posthumous hit with "Sitting on the Dock of the Bay," and Aretha Franklin added soul to Bacharach and David with the immaculate "I Say a Little Prayer." At the same time, Sly and the Family Stone defined the black music of the next decade in about three minutes when they released the epochal single "Dance to the Music."

Significant Albums and Singles of 1968

Albums: Rock

The Beach Boys: *Wild Honey*
Giving up on competing with the Beatles (or anyone else), the Beach Boys go for a soulful groove with mixed results. An "organic" direction that didn't last.

Big Brother and the Holding Company: *Cheap Thrills*
Janis Joplin brings blues and soul to hard rock. Super-fêted in its day for its heaviosity, the Joplin sound was soon to date.

The Byrds: *The Notorious Byrd Brothers*
More bogus ethnicity as über-folk rockers the Byrds turn themselves into a country band with the aid of country rocker Gram Parsons.

Chicken Shack: *Forty Blue Fingers Freshly Packed*
The British Blues Boom incarnate.

Cream: *Wheels of Fire*
George Harrison's best friend, Eric Clapton, and friends work hard on inventing rock, soloing, etc.

The Doors: *Waiting for the Sun*
The former pop idols continue their self-mythologizing.

Bob Dylan: *John Wesley Harding*
Recovering from a motorbike accident, Dylan discovers a new kind of roots music.

Fleetwood Mac: *Fleetwood Mac*
The Blues, featuring Peter Green's gorgeous guitar.

Jimi Hendrix: *Electric Ladyland*
The only truly innovative rock of the 1960s, performed by one of the few guitarists who could separate virtuoso playing from bluster.

Mothers of Invention: *We're Only in It for the Money*
A *Sgt. Pepper*-spoofing sleeve hides infantile wit and great playing skill. The Zappa cul-de-sac goes mainstream.

Love: *Forever Changes*
Creepy L.A. post-psychedelia at its orchestrated best.

The Moody Blues: *In Search of the Lost Chord*
Prog rock prepares to be born, but tunefully. Nice use of Mellotron.

Pentangle: *Pentangle*
Folkies feel safe to come out of the hand-tooled woodwork.

Pink Floyd: *Saucerful of Secrets*
The other great psychedelic band that recorded in Abbey Road begins its Syd Barrett-less voyage into mega-dinosauri-tudiness.

The Rolling Stones: *Beggar's Banquet*
Finally free of the Fab Four shadow, the Stones become the greatest rock 'n' roll band in the world etc.

Traffic: *Traffic*
Steve Winwood and friends go rural—and boring.

The Who: *The Who Sell Out*
The last great pre–Tommy gasp of the Who as pop art rockers. Wit was to vanish from their work for about the next three years.

ALBUMS: POP
Donovan: *A Gift from a Flower to a Garden*
Mister Rishikesh Folkie himself ploughs that acoustical furrow.

The Monkees: *Pisces, Aquarius, Capricorn and Jones Ltd.*
The greatest Beatles rip-off band begins to fall apart.

Simon and Garfunkel: *Bookends*
Before they would eat the world with *Bridge Over Troubled Water*, Simon and Garfunkel enjoy practice invasion of charts.

Various Artists: *The Original Cast of* Hair
The rock musical is invented.

Various Artists: *The Sound of Music (Soundtrack)*
What millions wanted in 1968.

ALBUMS: SOUL
Booker T and the MG's: *Soul Limbo*
Funky greatness from the band that would later record an instrumental version of *Abbey Road*.

James Brown: *Live at the Apollo Volume 2*
The Godfather, live and timeless.

The Four Tops: *Greatest Hits*
Motown at its most stentorian.

Otis Redding: *The Dock of the Bay*
Posthumous album from the inventor of pop soul.

SINGLES: ROCK
The Band: "The Weight"
Strange new music from bearded men. Soon, Paul McCartney would have a beard and a waistcoat too.

Cream: "Sunshine of Your Love"
Pop blues from Clapton and chums.

The Jimi Hendrix Experience: "All Along the Watchtower"
A Dylan cover so radical that Dylan himself would use Hendrix's arrangement from then on.

The Rolling Stones: "Jumping Jack Flash"
The Stones wake, as if from a dream, and remember who they are.

Canned Heat: "On the Road Again"
Bluesy drone pop at its finest.

Joe Cocker: "With a Little Help from My Friends"
The most excessive Beatles cover, with Jimmy Page on guitar.

Crazy World of Arthur Brown: "Fire"
A Novelty record the likes of which are not made nowadays.

Fleetwood Mac: "I Need Your Love So Bad"
Dreamy blues pop.

Manfred Mann: "The Mighty Quinn"
More Dylan covers.

The Nice: "America"
Emerson, Lake, and Palmer were just a breath away.

SINGLES: POP
Amen Corner: "Bend Me Shape Me"
Daft Brit bubblegum.

Louis Armstrong: "What a Wonderful World"
A gorgeous farewell from the king of a previous era.

The Beach Boys: "Do It Again"
Almost post-modern self-nostalgia from aging "surfers."

The Bee Gees: "I Gotta Get a Message to You"
One of the great pop bands makes a small but marvelous stop
on their epic voyage through 20th century music.

Cilla Black: "Step Inside Love"
Paul wrote this . . .

Bonzo Dog Doo-Dah Band: "I'm the Urban Spaceman"
. . . and produced this.

Dave Dee, Dozy, Beaky, Mick, and Tich: "Legend of Xanadu"
Weird S & M pop from a stupidly-named band.

Donovan: "Jennifer Juniper"
Charming, almost childish pop.

The Equals: "Baby Come Back"
Eddy Grant writes a rampaging pop soul classic.

Georgie Fame: "The Ballad of Bonnie and Clyde"
Bluesy MOR.

Bobby Goldsboro: "Honey"
Aptly-named sticky-sweet song about a wet woman.

Richard Harris: "MacArthur Park"
Deranged epic Jimmy Webb song that is mysteriously just
slightly shorter than "Hey Jude."

Mary Hopkin: "Those Were the Days"
Paul's protégé, folkie talent show winner, and, later, backing
vocalist on David Bowie's *Low* album.

Tom Jones: "Delilah"
Then as now, as over-the-top as an infantry charge.

The Moody Blues: "Nights in White Satin"
Yes, it is that old.

1910 Fruitgum Company: "Simon Says"
The true sound of pop in 1968.

Esther and Abi Ofarim: "Cinderella Rockefeller"
Mad, daft, and very engaging novelty pop.

Ohio Express: "Yummy Yummy Yummy"
More bubblegum, sexless and food-headed.

The Scaffold: "Lily the Pink"
Liverpool pop poets in number one shock. Hurray!

Simon and Garfunkel: "Mrs. Robinson"
Movie soundtrack hit for world-dominating pseudo-folkies.
They used to be called Tom and Jerry.

Dusty Springfield: "I Close My Eyes and Count to Ten"
Super-class pop from the blue-eyed soul queen.

SINGLES: SOUL

William Bell and Judy Clay: "Private Number"
Popular classic, full of the sex and rhythm of great Stax.

Aretha Franklin: "I Say a Little Prayer"
Bacharach and David go gospel, save world.

Marvin Gaye and Tammi Terrell: "You're All I Need to Get By"
Motown at its most seductive.

Sly and the Family Stone: "Dance to the Music"
The 1970s are about to be invented by the king of psychedelic funk. Probably the most important record of the year.

pop after the white album

"Suddenly you're 30 and there's still so much more to do."

John Lennon

THE WHITE ALBUM IS BY NO MEANS the most popular album of all time. It's a constant seller, but critically, it always just does pretty well in polls and top tens. Two recent polls—one for the Virgin *All Time Top 1000 Albums* book and the other, more sanely, for the British rock magazine Q's top 100 album list— place the White Album at five and six respectively, below albums by the likes of Radiohead (*The Bends, OK Computer*) and the Clash (*London Calling*). Other Beatles records such as *Revolver, Sgt. Pepper's Lonely Hearts Club Band*, and *A Hard Day's Night* usually place better too. The cable music channel VH-1 is similarly moderate, placing the White Album at 11 in its recent roundup, below a wider selection of music by Jimi Hendrix, Stevie Wonder, and even Nirvana (*Revolver, Sgt. Pepper*, and *Abbey Road* all come in higher than the White Album).

Nor can it be said that the White Album has exerted an enormous influence on rock music. While obviously excellent, eclectic, and beyond the abilities of most musicians and singers, it did not turn popular music on its head when it was released, and has consistently failed to do so since. Other Beatles records did do this. Singles such as "She Loves You," "Strawberry Fields," "Hey Jude," "We Can

Work It Out," and "I Am the Walrus" continually altered people's perceptions of what a pop song could be or do. Albums such as *With the Beatles, A Hard Day's Night, Rubber Soul, Revolver,* and *Sgt. Pepper* also turned the concept of the album upside down on an annual basis between 1963 and 1966.

It could be argued (by very ill people) that the White Album is a predictable set of songs that adds nothing to the Beatles' canon and is therefore inferior to most of its predecessors. In fact, while it is generally less of an innovator than the albums that came before it, the White Album is superior, as a set of songs, to many previous Beatles records. This is a highly subjective assessment, but not an absurd one. The Beatles, as a group, were at the height of their creative powers. Even as their interest in being the Fab Four waned, their skills did not. Right at the end of their career, in fact, on the *Abbey Road* album, they produced some of their best music. On the White Album, refreshed by India, free of drugs, and loaded up instead with acoustic guitar training and new melodies, the Beatles were able to present a whole slew of superb songs.

Equally, what the White Album has to offer that no other Beatles album does in such large measure is eclecticism, which in music translates as loads of songs written in different styles and drawn from any and every musical tradition. All Beatles albums are varied affairs: *Revolver* in particular ranges from children's songs to soul pastiches to ballads and back again. The White Album, however, makes a virtue of eclecticism. Starting with an obvious parody—the astounding "Back in the U.S.S.R."—the White Album ranges across the field of popular music like a lord surveying his lands. With its vast cornucopia of styles, the White Album suggests that the Beatles don't play pop music—they own it.

From the mutant ska of "Ob-La-Di, Ob-La-Da" to the avant-garde sound collage of "Revolution 9," from the 1920s flapper nonsense of "Honey Pie" to the proto-metal of "Helter Skelter," the White Album surveys the field of contemporary rock and pop and says: "I'll have some of that." Other bands might occasionally dare to pastiche some other kind of music. The Beatles just went in and grabbed it. Other Beatles albums are more experimental than this one, but on the White Album, the Beatles demonstrated that they could do anything; now they were just going to take pop and make it their own.

This is the legacy of the White Album, the gift it gave to popular music. It freed millions of bands from the tyranny of genre, the narrow-minded attitude that says, this band shall be a soul group and this band shall be a rock group. The White Album showed the world that pop music was for the taking, and the world never looked back.

the white album and charles manson

"I don't know, what's 'Helter Skelter'
got to do with knifing somebody?"

John Lennon

RECORDS MAKE AN IMPACT ON PEOPLE'S LIVES in different ways, but the White Album may be one of the few albums that is indirectly responsible for murder. The Beatles, with their fondness for word games, meaningless lyrics, and, at times, deliberate fan-baiting obscurity ("Glass Onion" is a song specifically designed to taunt fans), were so popular that almost every possible interpretation of their songs has cropped up at some time or other. Unfortunately, when the White Album came out, delighting the sane and entertaining millions, it was also freely available to the deranged and the psychotic, and became the album of choice for a Californian ex-con named Charles Manson.

Manson had spent most of his life in and out of prison, and in 1967, he found himself released into what must have seemed a new and promising world when he arrived in the Haight-Ashbury district of San Francisco. Haight-Ashbury was the very nexus of hippie, the place where the counter-culture invented itself on a pretty much hourly basis. In this environment, where anything went and where merely being an unusual character was enough to earn you a place in society, a person like Manson would easily find a new role.

His blend of charisma and nonsense soon found him a place in the new hippie community, for whom charisma and nonsense were a daily staple. Manson was a musician wannabe (although, sadly, the story that he auditioned for the Monkees isn't true), a songwriter, and a convincing speaker. He could take the most bizarre notions and make them seem feasible. (Not that this was a particularly hard thing to do in San Francisco in 1967, but even today, Manson remains a dangerously convincing and intelligent figure.) He also read the Bible constantly, which meant that his rhetoric was informed in a slightly different way than that of most of his contemporaries, who generally backed up their philosophizing with a bit of Eastern mysticism filtered through Timothy Leary.

Most of Manson's burgeoning gang of followers and hangers-on were continually stoned out of their minds, and Charlie naturally fell into the position of leader. He continued to write music, the lyrics of which were of a curiously negative nature, and his following grew. At a time when crime was considered vaguely revolutionary in underground circles, when the streets were full of unfocused, drug-addled middle-class youths, a figure like Manson—wild-eyed, intelligent, and, hey, a rock fan like the kids, was going to attract a lot of favorable attention. Under different circumstances (ones in which he was, say, sane), Charles Manson could have been a guru.

In the spring of 1968, Manson took his "family" in an old dilapidated school bus down to Los Angeles, where his freaks were welcomed with open arms by lots of other freaks. Future Blondie singer Debbie Harry almost made the ride, but decided against it at the last minute. The Family took refuge on a deserted ranch that had been used for filming westerns. It had fallen into disrepair, and its owner, George Spahn, let the Family stay there in return for errands and the various "favors" they would perform for him. The ranch was the perfect place for the Family: a community they could call their own. Charlie could practice his music to his heart's content, while at the same time feeding the damaged egos of his followers with his own drivel. At a time of astonishing uncertainty in the United States, to the Family, there was something reassuring about Manson. From a certain perspective, Charlie was right, and had all the answers. Most of the people on the Spahn Ranch were from privileged backgrounds, and misunderstood by their peers, thus finding comfort in this niche. The argument for Manson's popularity with the disenfranchised children of the middle classes goes something like this: imagine being told your entire life that you are worthless, and will never amount to anything. Cut to a few years later: you're stoned almost every day, sharing free love, listening to good music, and being told constantly that you are loved. It's not a ridiculous notion that people would gravitate to that kind of validation, and his followers were pleased to give him the devotion he commanded.

Tex Watson, a Family member widely believed to be Charlie's right-hand man, recalled the saloon within the faux western town that had been converted into a sort of nightclub. It was covered with Beatles posters, and decorated with lyrics from different Beatles songs, all written in luminous paint, lit with the mandatory ultraviolet light. The sheer mainstream-ness of the Beatles in this bizarre hippie cowboy environment wasn't that surprising. Part of the Beatles' extraordinary appeal was their ability to cross both sides of the tracks (they were probably the first group to go mainstream and then regain their underground following). Everybody loved the Beatles, from the hippies with their protest banners to the cops hitting the hippies with their nightsticks.

Apart from digging the Beatles, drugs were the Family's major pastime. Well, drugs, hanging out, and having sex—and in the Family, these weren't hobbies, they were daily tasks, broken up only by the occasional run to the big city to shoplift food, steal cars, and return with a feast from the dumpsters behind supermarkets. Then there was music. No other group of killers has ever been quite so closely associated with rock music. The Family made various musical contacts in Los Angeles, the most prominent of whom was Dennis Wilson, one of the Beach Boys. Dennis was pretty out there himself, always looking for the new experience, and he found it on the Spahn Ranch, which, for a good-looking, wealthy surfer dude like Dennis, was, essentially, hippie heaven. Manson had lots of girls who would do as he pleased, and he ordered them to literally charm the pants off Wilson. Dennis was also fond of Charlie's music, and arranged for a meeting with producer Terry Melcher, who was most known for his work with the Byrds and the fact that his mother was Doris Day. Charlie managed to cut a demo session with Melcher in hopes of cracking the music biz, but Melcher didn't see much promise in Charlie. Frankly, Charlie freaked him out. Melcher ditched Charlie, and Charlie became very, very bitter indeed.

Then a focus came for Manson's anger and apocalyptic worldview. Susan Atkins, a Manson follower whom he had nicknamed "Sadie Mae Glutz," recalled that in late 1968, Manson got a copy of the White Album, and brought it back to the ranch. The album made an incredible impact on their lives, so much so that Manson actually thought that the album "spoke to him." It helped things considerably that there was a song on the album called "Sexy Sadie," and that Manson had given Susan the "Sadie" nickname well before the album was released. No matter that the song was a veiled attack on the Maharishi Mahesh Yogi. Whenever the song "Sexy Sadie" came on, former stripper Susan/Sadie would dance, writhing in orgasmic fits, oblivious—like the rest of the world—to the subtleties of the lyrics.

Then there was "Helter Skelter." Dictionary definition— noun, a tower-shaped structure found at a fairground, with a spiral track outside it, down which people slide on a mat. According to Charlie, however, the concept was a little more complicated. His personal dictionary definition would have read: noun, the end of the world brought on by the Beatles. It is ironic and tragic that a song as unambiguous and meaningless as "Helter Skelter" would become the focal point for Manson's beliefs. His need to associate the band's music with the Bible would be so distorted that it would lead to at least seven pointless murders, and scare the bejesus out of everyone on the planet at some point in their lives. Manson had interpreted the song as a personal message to him from the Beatles to go out and start killing.

And then there was the Book of Revelations. Charlie became obsessed with the Book of Revelations, a book containing prophecies that, if your imagination is fluid enough, can be pretty much applied to anything. Satan is

Tinky Winky. Jesus Christ is Charles Manson. To the Family, that was just simply true, and Charlie didn't do a lot to discourage it. Even his surname got thrown into the mix. Manson. Man Son. Son of Man. Manson's obsession with the Book of Revelations was especially relevant to chapter 9. Revelations 9 sounds awfully like "Revolution 9." "Out of the smoke came locusts." Locusts—insects—beetles. the Beatles. It's obvious, if you're barking mad. "The four angels with breastplates of fire" were obviously the Fab Four and their electric guitars. "Their faces were like human faces, their hair like women's hair." Out of the mouths of the four angels "issued fire and brimstone," which would be their music. The four angels, who had been held ready for the hour, the day, the month, and the year, were released to kill a third of mankind. The very first verse of the chapter refers to a fifth angel, which logically would point to Stuart Sutcliffe, but because of the reference to having "power like scorpions"— and because Charlie was a Scorpio—Manson assumed that this clearly meant him. Charlie thought the Beatles were sending him a private personal message to "bring on Helter Skelter."

Tex Atkins remembers the Family being immersed in the White Album. It summed up pretty much most of their thinking, even if this thinking was filtered through Manson's own lyrical interpretations. He would preach for hours on end about "Helter Skelter," and how the Family would come out of the war as leaders. But Charlie's words were becoming more and more bitter. He started focusing his anger on the establishment. In this case, Harrison's bitter, unpleasant "Piggies" sent Manson a clear message. Manson thought the song criticized the unconcern of all the piggies to the situation around them. More ominous was the fact that Harrison had announced that they needed a "damn good whacking." To Manson and the Family, Helter Skelter was real. It meant that things were going out of control in the world, and it was going to end soon.

It should also be noted that the Family was a completely white group, and that black people were not welcome. Songs on the album such as "Rocky Racoon" became more significant to the Family than they would to almost anyone else. Manson himself explained the song to mean "coon," a derogatory term for black person. The song goes on to speak of Rocky's revival. Re-vival. The black man is going to come back into power again. Their call to "Rise" was clearly heard in "Revolution 9." Again, all of Manson's interpretations seemed to be backed up by the Book of Revelations. And then there was "Blackbird": "You were only waiting for this moment to arise" was clearly an invitation to black people to start an insurrection.

Listening to the White Album over and over again, in their drugged-out state, the Family's interpretations became even more bizarre. More and more "personal messages" in the White Album were becoming evident. In "Honey Pie," the Beatles were calling on Charlie to sail across the Atlantic, to be where he belonged. In "I Will," Charlie was told to sing loudly so they could hear him and be near him. But the song that really clinched the relationship was "Revolution 1." The lyric's mention of revolution and destruction fit snugly into Charlie's extremely elastic philosophy—that the time for peace and love was over, and now was the time for action.

Time for Armageddon. The fact that the Beatles wanted to hear "the solution" and "see the plan," was not a problem. Charlie had the plan. In "Revolution 9," he distinctly heard the Beatles say, "Charlie, send us a telegram." He just needed to talk with them. He made the call to the Beatles' offices from the ranch phone. The Beatles weren't in. At no point did Manson and his followers seem to ask themselves why the Beatles would go to the expense of recording an entire double album to send a secret message to a bunch of people in America. But then, conspiracies are so much more personal than stating the obvious.

While the Beatles were singing about the slide in "Helter Skelter" and how, when they got to the bottom they went back to the top, they may have thought they were making what John Lennon later described as "noise." Manson took this lyric as a reference to the bottomless pit in the desert where he and his followers would hide during the upcoming race war. When the black man became victorious, they would emerge from the hole. Another line in "Helter Skelter" apparently suggested a coded map to the exact location of this hole. (Quite how they were going to get out of a bottomless pit has never been explained.)

The central theme of Charlie's teaching became "Helter Skelter," the ultimate war between the blacks and the whites. The war would begin with a few incidents here and there (beginning in Los Angeles, where racial tension was already high after the 1965 Watts riots). As the Beatles sang, it was all "coming down fast." Not in a matter of years, but months, possibly even days. And Manson wanted to accelerate the process. The Family, meanwhile, believed what Charlie taught them to believe. It was their responsibility to bring on Helter Skelter by committing hideous crimes and make it look like they had been committed by black people. They would enter the piggy neighborhoods of Los Angeles—Bel Air and Beverly Hills—and perform horribly gruesome crimes on innocent people. They would leave evidence of the crimes in areas more populated with blacks, to lay the blame on them. The white establishment would be thrown into mass hysteria, and go on a rampage in the ghetto.

While this war was happening, the Family would be waiting in their "bottomless pit" in the desert, patiently looking forward to the day when they might emerge. The Family spent months in the desert looking for that hole, predictably with no success.

On August 8, 1969, Manson announced that the time for Helter Skelter had come. (Coincidentally, a few hours later that same day, the Beatles would be walking across the Abbey Road zebra crossing for the cover photo of their next album.) He ordered four of his closest and most trusted followers to go out and murder whoever was living in the house where Terry Melcher used to live. That night, there were five victims, the most prominent being actress Sharon Tate, the wife of Roman Polanski. Polanski was in Europe, and about to return to join his wife for the upcoming birth of their son in just two weeks' time. The five people in that house suffered horrible, tortuous deaths. When it was over, Atkins took a towel and dipped it in Tate's blood. She took the towel and wrote the word "PIG" on the front door.

The next night, Charlie sent another group out to a different area of L.A. That night a middle-aged couple were slaughtered in their own home. There was more writing: "Death to Pigs" on one wall, "RISE" on another, and on the refrigerator, the misspelled words "HEALTER SKELTER." They stole the wife's wallet and planted it in the restroom of a gas station a few miles away, in an area largely populated by blacks. They reasoned that someone would certainly find it, use the credit cards, and thus place the blame for the murders on the blacks. Fortunately, Helter Skelter, the war, never went any further than Manson's mind and these pathetic murders. The wallet was never found, and in the Family, paranoia was kicking in. Members were defecting and Charlie's world began to fall apart.

Susan "Sadie" Atkins was arrested for shoplifting and jailed. The proudest of the Family members, Sadie was still convinced the end of the world was nigh—she took it upon herself to warn her prison friends, and brag a little about the famous murders they committed. The five members of the Family directly involved with the murders, including Manson himself, were all convicted, and sentenced to die under the California law. When the verdicts were read, the Manson girls shouted at the judge and jury, "You have judged yourselves. Better lock your doors and watch your kids. Your whole system is a game, you blind, stupid people. Your children will turn against you." The death penalty in California was overturned shortly afterward.

The aftermath of the Manson murders is outside the scope of this book. Suffice to say that Charles Manson and his Family became the bogeymen for the bad end of the 1960s, the prototypical serial killers, and an easy watchword for horror-obsessed bands. From rock bands covering "Helter

Skelter" to singers naming themselves after Manson, it's bizarre that the White Album, originally conceived at a spiritual retreat in India by four men who believed in peace and love, should have become a symbol of murder, apocalypse, and hate.

The Beatles, understandably, were always reluctant to comment on the horror that Manson claimed they were responsible for unleashing. In 1970, Lennon took a distanced point of view, claiming that what Manson said in some respects was true—"He is a child of the state, made by us, and he took their children in when nobody else would." But he went on to say, reasonably enough, that Manson was "cracked, all right. . . . He's barmy, like any other Beatle fan who reads mysticism into it."

The Manson–White Album connection has always excited certain sections of the rock world. Songs from the White Album have a special resonance for these bands, and while no one has ever attempted a new version of, say, "Honey Pie" or—oddly—"Piggies," the album's most notorious rocker has attracted its share of attention. For a song that is some way from being great, "Helter Skelter" does well in the cover version stakes. The best version is by Siouxsie and the Banshees, the worst by U2, who covered it specifically to "take it back" from Charles Manson. Whether they succeeded or not, only time will tell.

Best known of the artists who explore the hypocrisy of modern society through their interest in the extreme—or, if you prefer, the "ooh, look at me" bands—is the singer Marilyn Manson (his real name is Brian Warner). His stage name is, of course, an amalgam of Marilyn Monroe and

Charles Manson (he could equally well have called himself Charles Monroe, but that wouldn't have sounded as dangerous). In 1992, Trent Reznor, former Marilyn Manson producer and leader of the industrial rock band Nine Inch Nails, rented the house where Sharon Tate was murdered. Despite looking at 15 houses that day before settling on it, Reznor denies that he knew the Cielo Drive house was connected with Charles Manson. The house was later demolished, but Reznor owns the front door (perhaps he didn't know that was connected with Charles Manson, either). These moments aside, the general interest in Manson has recently been confined to a small section of the cult rock fraternity, but it will doubtless resurface in a few years. It always does.

the beatles forever

"I'd like to end up sort of unforgettable."

Ringo Starr

THE WHITE ALBUM WAS BOTH A CRITICAL and a commercial success. It became the best-selling double album of all time for the next ten years, sold millions of copies, and spawned hits for countless other, lesser acts. Press coverage was generally extremely favorable. The *New Musical Express's* Alan Smith gave it a good review, pausing only to single out "Revolution 9" for criticism, calling the track "a pretentious piece of old codswallop." William Mann in the *Times*—the same William Mann who many years previously had referred to the Beatles' use of "Aeolian cadence" and "pandiatonic clusters"—referred to the White Album as "the most important musical event of the year." And, most famously of all, the album was reviewed in the *Observer* by Tony Palmer, filmmaker and controversialist. (The review is famous, by the way, because Derek Taylor—a smart PR man if ever there was one—reprinted the whole thing on the back sleeve of the *Yellow Submarine* soundtrack.) Palmer loved the album, calling it "a prolific out-pouring of melody, music-making of unmistakable clarity and foot-tapping beauty." (He also liked "Revolution 9" more than the *New Musical Express* did, claiming it was "janglings from the subconscious memories of a floundering civilisation.")

The Beatles, being the Beatles, moved along to the next stage of their career. Unfortunately, this was *Let It Be*. Week after week spent in the icy grimness of Twickenham Studios, film crews recording every frozen, out-of-tune moment, did nothing for the band's creativity. Nothing the ebullient McCartney could do made any (positive) difference. Lennon was more interested in Yoko Ono. Harrison was fed up with being told what to do. And Ringo wanted to be an octopus.

Despite various attempts to enthuse the band with the thought of live shows (something they hated), McCartney had to settle for a short performance on the roof of the Apple building at 3 Savile Row. The Beatles' last concert took place not in a desert at sunset or on an ocean liner, but on top of an office in London. The tapes of the *Let It Be* sessions were listened to by the Beatles, shelved, and passed on to the American producer Phil Spector.

Meanwhile, the band, as if to erase the memory of the whole *Let It Be* process, went back to George Martin to make another album. He insisted that this time there would be no nonsense about "getting back" to their roots; they would make a proper, well-crafted album with good songs and a real pop sheen to it. This they did, and the result was the Beatles' shiniest album yet, the super-pop *Abbey Road*, which, happily, featured Harrison's first single, "Something." The Beatles hired in Allen Klein to look after them, they all fell out, and, just to make things worse, *Let It Be* came out. Three weeks before that happened, McCartney decided to release his debut solo album, *McCartney*. Starr was sent to reason with him, and McCartney punched him.

Let It Be came out, smothered in Spector strings, half-filled with tatty jams and a desperate attempt at insouciance. Alan Smith at the *New Musical Express* called the album "a cheapskate epitaph, a cardboard tombstone, a sad and tatty end to a musical fusion which wiped clean and drew again the face of pop music." The Beatles broke up, and anyone who wanted to know why could go and see the movie of *Let It Be*, which had gone from being a study of a band entering "a new phase" to the now-classic documentary about a disintegrating rock group.

The Beatles' solo careers were, of course, by no means uneventful. Lennon became more public than ever; his and Ono's efforts to promote peace were roundly mocked by thousands, but no other rock star has ever devoted so much time to trying to change the world. His 1970s life passed through many different phases, and the music he made reflected that. There was the agitpop of *Some Time in New York City*—weak, issue-led rock music—and *Walls and Bridges*, which contains Lennon's best Lost Weekend song, "Nobody Loves You When You're Down and Out." There was the vague, nothing-to-say feebleness of *Mind Games* (don't be fooled by the fact that the single's good) and the drunken nostalgia of *Rock 'n' Roll*. And there were the great albums— *Plastic Ono Band*, where Phil Spector redeemed himself with a production that is both loud and sparse, and Lennon reached deep into himself for the best emotional songs of his, or anyone else's career; *Imagine*, which is the chocolate-box version of its predecessor; and, if your tastes veer toward the well-crafted and slightly comfy, the final peace of *Double Fantasy*. (Toward the end of his life, Lennon even revisited— musically, that is—his time at Rishikesh. One of his later demos was for a song called "The Happy Rishikesh Song," which suggests that the true secret of happiness is a woman.

The oddest thing about this song is that it has almost exactly the same tune as Harrison's solo song, "Blow Away.")

Lennon's murder in 1980 effectively canonized him, making a saint out of a far from saintly person. He had many faults, but the fact that Lennon has become a symbol of so many good things—truth, love, honesty, and peace—suggests that he was a man who the world has judged on his best actions.

Paul McCartney began the 1970s in a distinctly shaky fashion. Labeled the man who broke up the Beatles, and clearly the focus of the rest of the band's anger, McCartney faltered and stumbled time and time again. His early solo records—the excessively bitty *Wild Life*, the confused *Ram* and *Red Rose Speedway*—show a man who has lost confidence in himself as a writer. (Attacks such as Lennon's appallingly offensive "How Do You Sleep," with musical contributions from Starr and Harrison, can not have helped.) Later, with the help of his wife Linda and his musical collaborator Denny Laine, McCartney made the great *Band on the Run* and established Wings as a somewhat middle-of-the-road, but also sometimes surprising, pop group throughout the 1970s. In 1977, Wings' "Mull of Kintyre" became the best-selling U.K. single of all time, a record it held for fifteen years. The song was not released as an A-side in the United States.

After Lennon's death, McCartney disbanded Wings and successfully continued his career as a solo artist. He branched out into other fields—classical music, movie-making, painting—with differing degrees of success, and at the time of this writing, he continues to make excellent rock/pop records.

Linda McCartney's death in 1998 was a terrible blow to Paul McCartney. Linda's domestic and political influence on her husband was considerable. She helped him to become a vegetarian, and the McCartneys were prominent supporters of animal rights. Knighted in 1997, McCartney has always been the most active ex-Beatle.

Ringo Starr enjoyed a successful solo career in the early 1970s, at one point outcharting his former band colleagues. His limitations as a songwriter saw him at the mercy of the times, however, and various unsuccessful albums (some in the disco mode) ended his career before the 1970s were out. Starr suffered from drink problems for a time after this, but now he flourishes as an occasional actor and, best of all, as the narrator of the British children's TV show "Thomas the Tank Engine."

George Harrison was the ex-Beatle who initially benefited the most when the band split up. His debut solo album proper—*All Things Must Pass*—was a gigantoid boxed triple set that was swathed in one of Phil Spector's most epic productions. It sold by the continent-load, and set Harrison up for most of the 1970s. Harrison also organized the Concert for Bangladesh and continued to plough a spiritual furrow; unfortunately, his muse began to desert him in the 1970s, and this, combined with drink-related problems, seemed to suggest an end to his chart career. Harrison's abilities and prospects both rallied in the 1980s, however, and, with the aid of super-Beatle-wannabe Jeff Lynne of ELO, Harrison enjoyed more chart success in the 1990s. He was also one of the men behind Handmade Films, the company responsible for movies including Monty Python's *Life of Brian* and *Withnail and I.* He lost money when that company folded in the 1990s.

Harrison's final years—punctuated by cancer and a savage attack by a lunatic—were tragic ones. Rolling Stone and longtime friend Keith Richards believed that the knife attack ultimately contributed to Harrison's death. "What's unbelievable is the knifing, the attack at his home, is what did George in. I think he would have beaten the cancer if it wasn't for the blade," said Richards in 2001. "John and George—one by the gun, one by the knife. It's just that for such pleasant guys, who made such beautiful music and never did harm to anybody, to have to go through that kind of violence is puzzling to me." A less likely tribute came from Motorhead's Lemmy. "George Harrison really upset me. It was about three days before it really sank in. It was a real shame. He was the best musician in the Beatles and, in the end, he wrote the best songs. While Lennon and McCartney were off doing their personal columns, Harrison was coming out with great stuff." George's death in 2001 was made less unpleasant by his faith, and by his dry sense of humor. No one else would have had the last song they wrote published by a company called "RIP 2001 Music."

The Beatles finally began to mythologize and assess themselves in the 1990s, when the *Anthology* TV series, videos, and albums came out. At one point, this series would have been called "long-awaited," but so much time had elapsed since the project was first suggested that everyone had given up waiting. (The tangled situation with Apple did not help matters, nor did the Beatles' tense relationships; the series was to have been called *The Long and Winding Road*, but Harrison didn't want it named after a McCartney song.)

At the start of the 21st century, the Beatles are as popular as ever. New compilations—such as the *One* singles collection—come out from time to time, and go to number one all around the world, despite containing songs that are 40 years old. Beatles solo records including *Imagine, All Things Must Pass,* and *Band on the Run* have been remastered for CD. Even old cash-in collections like the "Blue" and "Red" compilations are hailed as rock classics. And actual Beatles albums from the time, such as the White Album, are dusted down, polished up, and brought out in new, improved editions. The Beatles will go on forever; and so long as they do, people will play the White Album, admire it, and love it.

acknowledgments

I'd like to thank Simon Huxstep for information about the Liverpool Scene, Tom Birch for his input on the White Album sessions, and my wife, Karen Krizanovich, for her suggestions, questions, encouragement, and ability to hear the White Album coming from another room for days on end. Scott Michaels provided all the information on Charles Manson in this book. His website, www.findadeath.com, is the best and funniest place to read about celebrity deaths.

The world is now fuller than ever with Beatles books, but there are still only two essential books for anyone fascinated with the work of the greatest group of all time: Mark Lewisohn's *Complete Sessions* and Ian MacDonald's *Revolution in the Head*. Unfortunately hard to find, Roy Carr and Tony Tyler's *The Beatles Illustrated Record* is one of the sharpest and best-looking critiques of the Beatles' career. Less reliably, the Internet is a fascinating place to find Beatles trivia (who else but a Nethead would devote time to a complete breakdown of the tape loops in "Revolution 9"?). Thanks to these sites, I now know what Prudence Farrow has been up to for the last 30 years, and I am filled with a sick, sneaking urge to hear Barbra Streisand's version of "Honey Pie."

This book was completed just after the death of George Harrison. The most underrated songwriter in the Beatles and, when on form, as good a composer as John Lennon and Paul McCartney, Harrison's best work was his life, his greatest achievement the dissemination of peace, love, and spirituality. He believed in reincarnation; I hope he's back soon.

index